How I
Pray Now

Bert Ghezzi

Fr. Michael Scanlan

Dan O'Neill

Babsie Bleasdell

John Michael Talbot

Bp. Joseph McKinney

Joe Pisani

Barbara Bartocci

Fr. Benedict Groeschel

Michael Garvey

Catherine Odell

Mike Aquilina

... and others

How I Pray Now

Edited by Jim Manney

Our Sunday Visitor Publishing Division
Our Sunday Visitor, Inc.
Huntington, Indiana 46750

855

Contents

Jim Manney — Introduction 7

1. **Bert Ghezzi** — With the Spirit 11

2. **Deborah Smith Douglas** — The River 17

3. **Father Raymond T. Gawrownski, S.J.** —
   Waiting 23

4. **Michael Garvey** — Like a Blind Beggar 28

5. **Babsie Bleasdell** — Blessings at Age
   Seventy-five 33

6. **Mike Aquilina** — With Difficulty 37

7. **Father Scott Seethaler, O.F.M. Cap.** —
   Honestly 42

8. **Lou Jacquet** — Late at Night 47

9. **Barbara Bartocci** — Letters to God 52

10. **Father Richard Antall** — Beads and Mysteries . 56

11. **Joe Pisani** — Without Ceasing 61

12. **Catherine Fournie**r — As an Adult Woman 67

13. **Christopher Bell** — My Anchor 72

14. **Bishop Joseph McKinney** — A Wildflower 77

15. **Sally Lynch** — Loss 82

16. **Dan O'Neill** — As the Bombs Burst 87

17. **Regina Doman** — Growing Up 91

18. **Father Giles Dimock, O.P.** — Finding Genuine
    Meditation 97

19. **Father Thomas Weinandy, O.F.M. Cap.** —
    Out Loud 102

20. **Henry Libersat** — In the Stillness 107

21. **Father Michael Scanlan, T.O.R.** — The Most
    Important Thing 112

22. **John Michael Talbot** — In the Desert 117

23. **Catherine Odell** — A Patchwork 123

24. **Father Benedict J. Groeschel, C.F.R.** — With a
    Broken Heart 127

Introduction

by Jim Manney

"… intimacy with God is at the heart of these stories."

L ooking back, it seemed like a can't-miss idea for *New Covenant* magazine. Let's ask a diverse and interesting array of people to write about their prayer life. Ask them *how* they pray, how their prayer has changed, what their problems with prayer have been. Call the series "How I Pray Now" and run it for a year or so. The readers are sure to love it.

I was the editor who thought up this idea. And I was right. The readers of *New Covenant* loved it. "How I Pray Now" has been one of the most popular features in the magazine's history.

But what looks like editorial acumen today seemed more like *chutzpah* when I asked Bishop Joseph McKinney to write the first article in 1994. Prayer is private, intimate. It's hard to write about. I thought I was being very bold when I asked people to publicly describe their relationship with God Himself. What would *I* think if an editor asked *me* to write about *my* prayer? I was ready for people to turn me down, muttering something about editors who don't think that even the sacred is sacred any more.

However, very few people turned me down. Most welcomed the opportunity to write about how they pray. Many commented that the experience was spiritually beneficial, a time to step back and think and reflect, and to thank God for all He had done to draw them closer to Him in prayer. They opened up their personal lives readily and most generously to the readers of *New Covenant*.

This ease and openness struck me as I read these articles again. For the men and women whose thoughts are collected here, prayer is a normal part of life. They get up in the morning and pray. They have a relationship with a Person. It has its ups and downs, its memorable moments and forgettable periods. Like all serious relationships, this one deepens and matures.

This is precisely the point many of these writers make so forcefully. A big difference between how they pray now and how they used to pray is their growing comfort with prayer — its normalcy. Many of these writers still struggle to pray regularly and cope with the practical challenges of finding a time and a place to pray. But for the most part these battles have been won. Their prayer life is one of the things they always do.

Nevertheless, it's not easy. The writers here are all busy people. They have full schedules of work and family commitments, friends to see, projects to complete, interests to pursue. Most are lay men and women. You'll find no monks here describing long peaceful hours of meditative walking and solitary contemplation in their cells. They make time and they grab time — rising early and staying up late, turning to God while commuting and doing errands, carving out quiet moments in the daily hubbub of work, school, and home life. One of the enduring challenges of how they pray now is continually adjusting their lives of prayer to the realities of a busy modern life.

What do people *do* when they pray? These articles are intriguing largely because they give us a peek at the actual content of this most intimate of relationships.

These writers do all sorts of things in prayer. Some say the Rosary, the daily office, the morning offering, "Come Holy Spirit," and other traditional Catholic prayers. Some pray with their pens as they write, with their voices in song and praise, with their prostrate bodies and upraised arms. Some are stirred by God's presence in nature; others by spiritual reading. Scripture is a very important component of their prayer lives. So is intercession for the needs of others.

However, the *doing* in prayer seems less important than the *being*. Many of us begin a commitment to regular prayer greatly concerned about what we do and how we do it. Here, there's a certain air of "been there, done that" about such matters — a mid-life perspective that ascribes greater importance to the quality of the relationship than to any particular thing that goes on within it.

The Curé of Ars once approached an old French peasant who spent whole days praying in the little village church. "What do you do?" the saint asked. "Well," said the peasant, "I look at Him and He looks at me."

This kind of intimacy with God is at the heart of these stories. The premise of *How I Pray Now* is that we pray differently now than we used to. There's a story to tell, and, indeed, these are love stories. These men and women write of falling in love with God, of growing tenderness and friendship, of understanding and being understood by the Person whose divine presence inflames their hearts. It is supremely inspiring to me to know that this is how so many Catholics today pray now. May these stories inspire your efforts to grow in your life of prayer.

1

With the Spirit

by Bert Ghezzi

"The mystery of Christian prayer stuns me. I am praying in Christ and Christ is praying in me."

In his "Confession," St. Patrick commented on the spirituality of his late middle-age. "My love and fear of God," he said of his youthful prayer, "increased greatly, and my faith grew, and my spirit was stirred up. . . . Nor was there any tepidity in me, such as I now feel, because then the spirit was fervent within me." Like all who may discover that their youthful fervor has strangely cooled, I find Patrick's admission of weakness encouraging.

I confess that occasionally I also feel some tepidity in my spirit, and I'm tempted to tell you that my prayer is usually just workmanlike and sometimes downright ho-hum. Rarely does it zing and pop with enthusiasm. But that would be misleading because it might make it seem that I find my personal worship tiresome. Not so. I really enjoy all my daily morning quiet times with God, and find them spiritually enriching.

Years ago, I stopped evaluating my prayer or even thinking about it much. So dryness and distractions don't discourage me anymore. I don't let them. C. S. Lewis's wise devil, Screwtape, taught me that God regards most highly the prayer we offer when we feel least like praying.

"Well, that was pretty lousy," I might have once said about an especially dull prayer time. But not recently. Now I know that God has quite a different perspective on my prayer: He appreciates all my dogged efforts to worship Him. Maybe I am distracted, maybe I don't feel very spiritual, but I'm confident that the Lord values my freely choosing to spend time praying, even when I don't think I'm doing it very well. So a prayer that I see as ho-hum might zing and pop for Him, a Father delighting in His son's stick-to-it-iveness.

The mystery of Christian prayer stuns me. When I worship with the community at Mass or personally at home, I remind myself that I am praying with Jesus. By the working of the Holy Spirit, I tell myself, I am praying in Christ and Christ is praying in me. That reality makes a huge difference in my worship.

Clifford Howell, a great Jesuit precursor of the liturgical renewal, used to say that before our baptism, we could only pray with "one humanpower." But with the Spirit in us, he said we could pray with "one Godpower," an immeasurably better way to worship. So at the start of my prayer I deliberately plug myself into the source of divine power. "O Lord, open my lips, and my mouth shall declare your praise," I say, inviting the Lord to rev me up and unite me to His perfect prayer.

More than ever, the Mass and the sacraments are at the heart of my personal worship. No matter how dull the homily, no matter how lifeless the participation, no matter how insipid the music, I never leave Sunday worship disgruntled or disappointed. I decided long ago that I would not expect to get anything *out* of Mass. Rather, I would strive to put everything *into* Mass, giving my all with Christ to God in the Eucharist. With that perspective, my Sundays are usually upbeat, and I find that the Spirit of the liturgy spills over into my daily prayer.

Thirty-five years ago I learned to pray by reciting and reflecting on the psalms. The themes of these Bible prayer songs are now imbedded in my brain, and I repeat them spontaneously.

Sometimes their words fill me with wonder and their cadences draw me near to the Lord. "Your mercy, Lord, towers above the heavens," I pray, awestruck, realizing the psalmist who wrote that verse had no idea how vast the universe really is. Or in the psalmist's voice, I ask, "Who am I, God, that You even think of me, one among billions of Your creatures? But You have put me first in Your thoughts, so I put You first in mine."

To keep the psalms fresh in my heart, at morning prayer I still use two popular versions of the Liturgy of the Hours that a friend gave me twenty years ago.

Lately, I have built my personal worship around several traditional Christian prayers, including the Sign of the Cross and the Lord's Prayer. I have rediscovered the simple power of making the Sign of the Cross. When I sign myself, I do it reflectively, professing faith in the Trinity, acknowledging that I died and rose with Christ in my baptism, marking myself as belonging to Christ and defending myself against the enemy. I even do it in public, especially when I am navigating Florida's devilish traffic.

Last year, I took some time to study the Our Father, seeking to unpack its meaning. I read books about it and consulted the new *Catechism of the Catholic Church*. Now I often spend a whole prayer time reflecting and extemporizing on the petitions of the Lord's Prayer.

My study has always enhanced my prayer. During the last year, for example, I have been reading lives of the saints. Thinking about these great pray-ers has enlivened my spirituality. From Francis Xavier I learned to surrender to God; Teresa of Ávila showed me that it's never to late to grow in prayer; and St. Patrick, bless him, assured me that it's okay to feel tepid in my late middle-age. I also find it helpful to model my prayer on prayers of the saints. Often I use with great benefit St. Patrick's breastplate prayer — "Christ be with me, Christ before me. . . ." or St. Francis of Assisi's Praises of God — "You are my love, you are my wisdom. . . ."). And one of my favorites is this gem from St. Thomas Aquinas: "Pour out now, I beg you, a ray of your clear light upon my murky understanding and take from me my doubly dark inheritance of sin and ignorance." Ah, yes Lord, just a tiny flash of Your light today would be enough to do the trick.

Intercession is always part of my morning prayer time. I remind the Lord that I expect Him to save and sanctify my wife and family, naming each one and citing their special needs. I also pray for a long list of relatives, friends, and ministries. My study of John's Gospel several years ago persuaded me that God always says yes to my prayers for the salvation of family and friends. In fact, I believe that He cannot say no to such a prayer, for doing so would contradict His nature and His purpose. John declares that what God is all about is begetting for Himself a family of sons and daughters. That's why He created human beings in the first place. So I am confident that He wants all of us in His divine family, desiring it even more than I do. And I want nothing more. Knowing that makes my intercessory prayer more rewarding, even fun.

St. Teresa of Ávila confessed that she dabbled in prayer for twenty years before she got serious. The turning point for her came when a spiritual director asked her to pray daily the *Veni, Creator Spiritus*. Since I yearn to pray better, I have been imitating her example, concluding my daily prayer with that ancient invocation of the Holy Spirit. I expect Him to help me pray with even more Godpower than ever.

Veni, Creator Spiritus

Come, Creator, Spirit, come
from your bright heavenly throne,
come, take possession of our souls,
and make them all your own!

You who are called the Paraclete,
best gift of God above,
the living spring, the vital fire
sweet christ'ning and true love!

You who are sev'nfold in your grace,
finger of God's right hand;
his promise, teaching little ones
to speak and understand!

O guide our minds with your blest light,
with love our hearts inflame;
and with your strength, which ne'er decays,
confirm our mortal frame.

Far from us drive our deadly foe;
true peace unto us bring;
and through all perils lead us safe
beneath your sacred wing.

Through you may we the Father know,
through you, th'eternal Son,
and you, the Spirit of them both,
thrice-blessed Three in one.

All glory to the Father be,
with his co-equal Son;
the same to you, great Paraclete,
while endless ages run. Amen.

Adapted from Hymns for the Year (1896),
translator anonymous

You are holy, Lord, the only God
and your deeds are wonderful
You are my love,
You are my wisdom,
You are my strength
You are my humility,
You are my endurance,
You are my rest,
You are my peace.
You are my faith
My great consolation,
You are my eternal life,
Great and wonderful Lord,
God almighty,
Merciful Savior. Amen.

Adapted from "Praises of God,"
by St. Francis of Assisi

Christ, be with me, Christ before me, Christ behind me,
Christ in me, Christ beneath me, Christ above me,
Christ on my right, Christ on my left,
Christ where I lie, Christ where I sit, Christ where I arise,
Christ in the heart of everyone who thinks of me,
Christ in the mouth of everyone who speaks of me,
Christ in every eye that sees me,
Christ in every ear that hears me.
Salvation is of the Lord.
Salvation is of the Lord,
Salvation is of the Christ.
May your salvation, Lord, be with us always. Amen.

From St. Patrick's Breastplate

Bert Ghezzi, father of six adult and teenaged children, is a book editor, magazine columnist, and author. He lives in Winter Park, Florida.

2

The River

by Deborah Smith Douglas

"Sometimes my prayers for others have no words at all, merely a sense of lifting those I love or ache for into God's infinitely compassionate hands."

H ow do you pray now?" I like the question. It implies change; it implies that prayer — like any other profound, committed, intimate relationship — is *will* change, will grow and develop in response to changing circumstances. Like the Santa Fe River near where I live, our prayer sometimes overflows its banks, sometimes diminishes to the merest life-sustaining trickle, sometimes cuts a whole new course in the landscape.

The question "How do I pray now?" has been for me an invitation to get, as it were, an aerial view of the river; a chance to look down and see the riparian loops and bends, the shallow places and the rapids, the floodplains and the dams. It is all the same river — I can see that clearly from this airborne vantage point: the continuity, so often hidden in the small view of daily life, is revealed. And my river, while sometimes dallying in near-stagnation, sometimes choked by debris, sometimes even appearing to flow backward, continues stubbornly to seek the sea.

This continuity in my prayer life is perhaps most apparent in its external forms. For more than a decade, most mornings I have risen early for a quiet time before the crowded day begins. I participate in the community prayer of the Eucharist at least once a week; I am grateful for annual retreats; volunteer service to the larger community keeps me balanced and connected to the world; and regular conversations with my spiritual director provide invaluable clarity and support.

All of these spiritual disciplines are important to me; none is dispensable. It is in the totality of them, woven together, that my life in God is sustained. Interior prayer without corporate worship tends toward self-preoccupation, and without guidance tends toward self-delusion; service without a faith context becomes "dead works." Nevertheless, it is the daily private prayer that I would like to look at now — partly because it is the anchor for so much else, and perhaps also because it is the part that has undergone the most change, and changed the most significantly, over the course of the years.

Twenty years ago I was in law school, where I systematically (painfully) trained my somewhat dreamy English-major mind to jump through hoops of adversarial argument and method. It has taken me a long time to recognize — much less to undo — the damage this hard-won way of thinking did to my praying. For many years, I (unconsciously, of course) treated prayers as legal briefs, or at least as business letters ("Holy and Ever-living God, Dear Sir:"). Sometimes I prayed as though I were an attorney presenting a case before the Divine Judge, seeking by my eloquence, my logic, my sure grasp of the issues, and keen sense of justice, to persuade the heavenly court to a certain course of action. Sometimes I prayed as though I were the firm's efficient executive secretary, bringing urgent lists and messages to the attention of the overworked senior partner who, without my help, could hardly be expected to establish priorities or even to recognize crises.

These days, by the grace of God, my prayer has changed. I pray, these days (ever so tactfully) with much less conviction of my own importance in setting an agenda for God's busy day, and with much more of an awestruck sense of the great privilege of simply participating in God's eternal love, letting it shine through my life as unobstructed as possible, like sunlight through clear glass. In other words, I seek now not so much to be the Supreme Court's star turn as — in the words of George Herbert — "to be a window, through God's grace."

Consequently, my prayers of intercession are much more trusting and quiet, much less insistently partisan and vocal, than once they were. When I remember before God the pain of the world, I am less concerned with verbal eloquence than I used to be, much less implicitly sure that my job in prayer is somehow to change God's mind. In fact — except for the Collect for Purity at the beginning of my prayer time and the Lord's Prayer at the end — sometimes my prayers for others have no words at all, merely a sense of lifting those I love or ache for into God's infinitely compassionate hands.

It is not only the shape of my intercessory prayer that has changed with time, but also the way I pray with Scripture. As a Protestant born and bred, I have always been deeply aware of the importance of the biblical revelation of God's purpose for human life. "Bible Study" and "Bible School" were part of my life from the time I could read. By the time I was eight, I could recite all the books of the Bible in order, from Genesis to Revelation. I had memorized several psalms in their entirety, and could quote chapter and verse for most of the more memorable promises in Scripture. On my wedding day, I carried a white leather-bound Bible, a gift from my mother, along with my bridal bouquet. When I began the practice of daily prayer, I brought not only the Bible into the morning quiet, but also *Strong's Exhaustive Concordance* and *Peake's One Volume Commentary* — a well-intentioned but unwieldy lapful that pretty effectively ensured that my praying with Scripture would stay firmly in my head, far more intellectual and cognitive than meditative or receptive. I learned a great deal during this time in my life, but it was much ado about critical method and hermeneutics, and had precious little to do with listening for the Word of God in my own experience.

It has taken our patient God years to open my heart and quiet my endless earnest picking-apart of holy writ. More than any other single factor in this transforming of my scriptural prayer, a graced experience of Ignatian spirituality helped me to glimpse the possibilities of praying with imagination and heart as well as with intellect.

It was a week of special blessing; the depth and power of the meditations quite took my breath away. As a Christ-centered, biblically grounded Protestant with years of the gentle discipline of *lectio divina* behind me, I thought I knew — thought I had always known — what it means to "pray with Scripture," but I was wrong. Unconsciously but inevitably, I was limiting the operation of divine grace to the Calvinist dictum of *scriptura sola*, clinging stubbornly to the written word in a way that kept the Living Word from entering my heart. Under the wise guidance of my Jesuit director, in the blessed quiet of the place, by the grace of God, I was led that week to a whole new understanding of "real presence" in scriptural prayer — a radically sacramental sense of actual encounter with Christ, who is "in, with, and under" the narrative.

Needless to say, that retreat has profoundly influenced "how I pray now." When I compose myself to reflect, in the presence of God, on a passage in Scripture, I am no longer seeking the definitive scholarly interpretation of the text: instead, I am offering my whole self — imagination, memory, intellect, desire

— to the whispered Word of God. I am open to divine surprises; I let the river go where it will.

These, then, are two specific ways in which the way I pray now has deeply changed from the way I used to pray: when I intercede for others, I am more offering myself to be an instrument of God's peace than I am lobbying for a particular result; when I pray with Scripture, I am offering myself to the Living Word rather than clinging to the written word. "Offer" seems to be the operative verb here — more and more, my prayer is more listening than talking, more giving than asking.

Consequently — back to the river again — the way I pray is increasingly "without ceasing," as silent, steady, and active as a river flowing through the land.

Langston Hughes speaks of this transforming dynamic at the very heart of who we are in his poem "The Negro Speaks of Rivers":

> I've known rivers;
> I've known rivers ancient as the world
>   and older than the flow of human blood in human
>   veins.
> My soul has grown deep like the rivers.
> I bathed in the Euphrates when dawns were young.
> I built my hut near the Congo and it lulled me to sleep.
> I looked upon the Nile and raised the pyramids above it.
> I heard the singing of the Mississippi when Abe Lincoln
>   went down to New Orleans, and I've seen its muddy
>   bosom turn all golden in the sunset.
> I've known rivers:
> Ancient, dusky rivers.
> My soul has grown deep like the rivers.

I would like to think that my soul has — once and for all — "grown deep like the rivers," that my prayer, my whole life in God, has reached a place of permanent quiet depth and power beyond change. I know it is not so: it is not in the nature of rivers not to change, and I am sure God is not finished with me yet. But I do hope that God will give me the grace not to struggle against the changes too much, not to rush in — self-willed as the Army Corps of Engineers — to build dams or embark on diversion schemes. I hope I can stay open to the Spirit of God in my listening, and always trust in the limitless and everlasting sea toward which, however slowly, I still wind my way.

I love Ezekiel's vision of the sacred river that flows from the throne of God, deep and mighty, "a river I could not pass through, for the water had risen; it was deep enough to swim in." Wherever the river goes, it gives life: "when it enters the stagnant waters . . . the water will become fresh . . . *everything will live where the river goes*" (Ezekiel 47:5, 8-9). I thank God for the river that runs through all of life, for waters that baptize us ever deeper into the new creation, for prayer that is alive, and "deep enough to swim in."

Deborah Smith Douglas is a writer and attorney living in Santa Fe, New Mexico.

3

Waiting

by Father Raymond T. Gawrownski, S.J.

*"I wonder if there is a prayer of the middle-aged
and balding, a time in which it is enough to just
sit and be, in quiet trust."*

oday, as I write this, I have been a priest for nine years, a member of a religious order for twice that length of time. I wonder if there is a prayer of the middle-aged and balding, a time in which it is enough to just sit and be, in quiet trust. There is little to say much of the time: how often can one repeat things I have told Him? And by now, I trust that He knows all about me, all that has been, all that will be. Of course, there are times when particular needs come to the surface, and my prayer becomes that of a child: "Oh please, please, please. . . ." And now and then I sit down and say, "Thanks, thanks, thanks," for all those prayers answered over the years.

It is more like a constant mindfulness that I plug into in particular periods of prayer, as if, as St. Paul writes, it is the Spirit praying in and through me, rather than so much I who am bringing myself to prayer. Yes, I exist; yes, I, this person and no other, as I go through my daily rounds and adventures and periods of ennui, I have this unique "take" on reality. And yet, there is a deeper current at work here, one that flows under my words, my thoughts, under the often chaotic cell that is my heart.

For a long time my prayer was very much in that heart. The great gift of religious life was having time to pray and having the freedom to move down from the cerebral regions, from the "talking head" and rediscovering the heart. It was the freedom the Lord gave me — no small gift for an intellectual — to just say to people "I don't know" instead of having to chatter all the time.

That move to the heart was tied, for me, to a real homecoming that began in my late twenties, a return to my roots — quite literally, an adult rediscovery of family, of the happy memories of childhood and young life so often obscured in the turbulence of young adulthood and the revolutionary waves that have swept over our lives since the late 1960s. That meant literally coming home as well as, in terms of prayer, moving into the very center of my being and taking up residence in my heart.

For a long time my prayer was just the joy of moving into my heart and sitting there. Sometimes the Lord would visit me there; we might chat. Of course, the world would intrude, and my own passions would be roused to murkiness by anxiety, anger, resentment, or other desires: the "cares and riches and pleasures" (Luke 8:14) of which Our Lord warns us. But the storms would pass and calm, clear days would return and azure evenings in which I would sit with the Lord as cozily in the depths of my heart as every hobbit did in his hobbit hole.

So it was for a number of years. At times I would be lifted up, as when praying with a holy soul, or as when I found myself in one of the gorgeous Russian liturgies I used to be part of in the nine years I was actively involved in the Russian rite.

Then big changes came to my life. I was sent to a new city where I no longer had access to that Russian rite. The life of graduate studies that had allowed me much time for inwardness gave way to the far more extroverted life of a professor, lecturing nine hours a week before one hundred twenty students. It was as if I had to leave my beloved home and head into a foreign country for work.

And then came the biggest challenge of my life. Last autumn, word came that my very active mother had suffered a severe stroke. I rushed to her bedside and stayed there as, day by day, we hoped for some sign of recovery. Instead, on the feast of the Immaculate Conception, a shocked family doctor told us that a routine test had revealed a metastatic cancer, far advanced, and that there really was no earthly hope.

So I sat by her side and prayed with her until her death on the feast of the Presentation, as she received the Holy Eucharist during Mass. I have no doubt that the Lord took care of her — and us — all those months, and that He took her to Him. But I also feel that somehow I died at that time as well, or at least so much of me that I am not yet quite resurrected. After we buried our mother, the home to which I had returned was gradually stripped and put up for sale, and one day I got into an airplane and left forever.

That was four months ago. Now I pray for life, for new life, for resurrection after the storms of this past winter. It is as if I have moved through my own heart to a new life in Christ, dwelling more and more in Him. My prayer now is a prayer of watching, of being, of sitting. Sometimes I rise in the night and sit before the Blessed Sacrament. Perhaps that is the single greatest development in my prayer: my need to be with Our Lord in the Blessed Sacrament is far greater than it ever was before. It is just a sitting in love, a becoming very quiet and calm and letting a circulation of love move around my heart from the heart of God. Sometimes people come to mind and I share them with God — or He shares them with me: we share them, which is good, for He can do far more for them than I.

There are other sorts of prayer times as well. Sometimes I love to sit with the Scriptures open on my lap. I have a beautiful leather-bound Bible, and it consoles me to just have it like a child on my knees, and I find joy in reading the psalms. Sometimes I long for God, for He seems so distant from the world in which I live, and sometimes so far from me. Sometimes, I find company in the penitential psalms, knowing that I am a sinner, blind, foolish, miserable — and yet one with all such wretches who have been called by the One who knew us before we were born, and whose love is really the only reason to go on through the murkiness of our days.

I try to pray my daily Rosary, and lately have been trying to be more mindful of Our Lady as my mother, as a real person to whom I am praying instead of a benign figure to whom one rattles off vocables. And sometimes I just breathe Hail Marys when I think of people in need, or people for whom I might worry, or people whom I dislike, or whom I have wronged.

At times while hearing a confession, I am lifted to a wonderful prayer of adoration and humility to God, for seeing the beauty of another soul is a privilege that can open the floodgates of the heart. And as a priest of God, I think I pray best when I disappear at the altar and let the Divine Bridegroom breathe through me to His Beloved, the Church, gathered before me, with all her needs, cares, agendas, and underlying all, the one great sigh of the human heart for her Lord and Maker.

In the early years there was much more going on in me emotionally; there was much more a palpable warmth of the heart and sometimes sweet tears. Now, in my middle years (as I have moved to the Midwest as well), I find more a quiet waiting, for the little epiphanies I once knew must recede to make way for the great wave that is no doubt coming one of these days, when all the flesh and life's display will recede to make way for the tidal wave of His love, which is one way I think of the Resurrection.

In this meantime, I trust Him to lead me through all the scenes in which I find myself, and hope that somehow His glory is being served. When I think of it, I thank Him and praise Him as I go along, for the further I go, the more I sense that I am living the life of Jesus in the world today, or perhaps rather that He is living His life in and through me. That does not mean that I cease to be me, and I come to Him in confession to receive and acknowledge His great generosity to me — but it means that somehow I do not matter so very much anymore. I just try not to get in His way, both in serving His people and in sitting before His tabernacle in the quiet hours when He calls me there, "waiting in patient hope."

Father Raymond T. Gawrownski, S.J., is assistant professor of Scripture at Marquette University in Milwaukee.

4

Like a Blind Beggar

by Michael Garvey

"Even my boring, carping, wheedling, prissily recited prayers are pleasing to God."

I can't honestly write about how I pray now without making a couple of humdrum confessions, so please permit me: I often pray the Rosary when driving alone. Recently, while waiting at an unusually busy intersection, I allowed my attention to ricochet from the Joyful Mystery of the Visitation to the infuriatingly hesitant redneck immediately in front of me in the left turn lane. He was one of those feloniously obstructive drivers who refuse to pull into the center of the intersection, thus imposing on the three or four cars behind him a long and unreasonable wait for the next green light.

If such drivers could be prosecuted, I would be in favor of capital punishment; if they could be positively identified in their prenatal state, I would be moderately pro-choice; and if they could be gathered into one, geographically isolable nation, I would advocate a first strike with nuclear weapons. Which is all a way of explaining why I interrupted my prayer with a few bellowed words which, to put it mildly, did not praise the Son of God and the Son of Mary, albeit they were addressed neither to Jesus, nor to His mother, but to a fat guy in a red Oldsmobile.

Even more recently, while on vacation with my family in a Lake Michigan resort town, I was at Mass one morning at a parish whose people were enthusiastically celebrating the twenty-fifth anniversary of the Diocese of Kalamazoo. In the middle of the liturgy of the Eucharist, at the Consecration, as we all beheld bread and wine in a priest's hands becoming Jesus' own body and blood and soul and divinity, I realized that I was trying to remember the tune and rhythm of that delightful alphabetical jingle at the conclusion of the Glenn Miller song "I Got a Gal in Kalamazoo."

When I was a little boy preparing for my first communion, I was moved by the stories the Dominican sisters told us about how His best friends had fallen asleep while a terrified Jesus was fretfully praying, awaiting His arrest, disgrace, imprisonment, torture, and execution. Some friends, I used to think. Occasionally, I continue to indulge that unexamined indignation when the apostles' successors so conspicuously fall asleep, but I shouldn't. I fall asleep every bit as often as the worst bishop does.

So how do I pray now? I'm afraid the above stories are fairly characteristic. I pray badly, I suppose, although it's hard for me to imagine what it would mean to pray "well." I love the definition of prayer as "keeping company with God," and anybody who has been married for a while knows what a mysterious thing it is to keep company with someone you love and who loves you. It's less a matter of performance than of commitment.

What I first must do is accept and receive a promise to stay with a Person, and that requires all the most important things persons do, like listening, speaking, remembering, enjoying, fearing, forgetting, quarreling, forgiving, and being forgiven, among many other things. It's less a matter of what I feel than what I do.

So what I do is stay. I try to be faithful to my Lord, longing for His approval and attending Him in fits and starts, and all too often falling asleep with the apostles, all too often spoiling my efforts at showing Him my love with instances of rage, cowardice, pride, lust, and just plain meanness.

I try to remember at such times the blind beggar Bartimaeus (in Mark 10:46-52), outside Jericho, who kept ignoring the perfectly sane suggestion to hang it up and accept his handicap. He kept on screaming "Son of David, have mercy on me!" until Jesus heard him over the crowd noise, stopped, pitied him, restored his sight, and let him follow. And this is the very same Jesus who said that to cry "Lord, Lord" was insufficient to gain access to His kingdom.

I obviously don't understand this contradictory Jesus very well, and, frankly, I mistrust most of those who want to explain Him to me. But in the meantime, the prayer of Bartimaeus makes the most sense to me. No matter how sterile and perfunctory my prayer is, I cannot bring myself to believe that it is not, on some level, worth the effort, that even my boring, carping, wheedling, prissily recited prayers are pleasing to God.

I will be forever — I hope literally — indebted to a wonderful Benedictine monk who, when I was a teenager, taught me about the Jesus Prayer ("Lord Jesus Christ, Son of God, have mercy on me, a sinner.") and who encouraged me to recite it over and over again, and who told me not to worry about the fact that it often seemed that I was praying to a void.

When I say the Rosary and hear the tedium of the Hail Marys dully reverberating in my heart and lungs like the base line of a bagpipe, I often have that terrible sense of futility. Or when I say an Our Father with my kids before bedtime, or make a knee-jerk Sign of the Cross, or kneel down in front of a tabernacle and absolutely nothing seems to happen within or without me, I'm tempted to take the advice of the people who surrounded Bartimaeus and told him to hush up, implying that he would always be this way, blind, miserable, and abandoned.

But just as a distracted and dutiful kiss between spouses can enact and foreshadow the most profound embraces of their marriage, these formulaic gestures and utterances can become moments of real grace. Besides, when your attention span is as short and feeble as mine, you find yourself clinging to ritual as tenaciously as a drunkard to a lamppost.

All of us in the Church are exhorted to "pray without ceasing," and I know I am a long way from that, but I do try to pray whenever I remember that exhortation, and I pray for the grace to remember it much more often. Sometimes I know I have convinced myself that I am praying when I am actually daydreaming, talking to myself, and not at all to God.

Bruce Jay Friedman's iconoclastic and under-appreciated play, "Steambath," has an arresting illustration of this sort of thing. The play involves several characters who find themselves in an odd sort of health club awaiting the judgement of God, who has mysteriously revealed Himself as a Puerto Rican steambath attendant.

The play ends frighteningly as the main character adamantly places himself beyond the reach of God's mercy, outraged at this divine failure to behave predictably, and refusing to let a loving God get a word in edgewise, continually preempting his own redemption by insisting, "I know what you're going to say . . . ." In a televised version that I saw some time ago, the camera pans back as God, who has become increasingly silent, increasingly excluded, seems to disappear from the play, leaving this fatuous man alone and damned.

When I think of this, I sometimes think that I say the Our Father a bit too casually, especially when I ask that God deliver us from evil. I tend to forget how much the evil from which I ask Him to deliver us is the evil within me, evil with which I've grown quite comfortable, evil which leads me to believe that I already know what He is going to say, that I have no need of Him. And then once more I pray the prayer of the blind beggar of Jericho, "Son of David, have mercy on me."

And then I wait for the miracle to happen.

Michael Garvey is assistant director of public relations at the University of Notre Dame.

5

Blessings at Age Seventy-five

by Babsie Bleasdell

"Even at age seventy-five, I don't know what God will do next. All I know is that when He is doing it, I want to be there."

Every New Year's Day I make a resolution. In all my years — and I turned seventy-five this year — I can't truthfully say that I have lived out any resolution beyond a month or two. This year has been different so far. In the first reading on New Year's Day the Lord said to Moses, " 'Say to Aaron and his sons, Thus you shall bless the people of Israel: you shall say to them, The LORD bless you and keep you: The LORD make his face to shine upon you, and be gracious to you: The LORD lift up his counte-nance upon you, and give you peace' " (Numbers 6:22-26). When I heard that, I thought, I can make a resolution to bless. It is the one resolution in my seventy-five years that I have not broken. In fact it has increased, the blessing becoming not only part of my prayer, but a way of greeting people as well.

Changes like this, both large and small, are a constant part of my prayer life, and, I'm certain, of yours. Through the years, as we pray, the Holy Spirit sensitizes us to the heart of Jesus; our heart picks up His burden. Taking on this burden is very difficult for me, especially when I must be with people who are a real trial. But Mother Teresa has a prayer that I've learned by heart and whisper all day long, especially when I'm having dif-ficulty with people. It says, "Mary, Mother of Jesus, give me your heart, so beautiful, so pure, so immaculate, so full of love and humility that I may be able to receive Jesus in the Bread of Life, love Him as you love Him, and serve Him in the distress-ing disguise of the poorest of the poor."

I realized as I began to pray it, that contrary to my thoughts, the poorest of the poor weren't necessarily the vagrant on the street, the homeless, or the addict. The poorest of the poor were people, who may be quite rich in everything, but whose pres-ence or attitude is really difficult. I began to put people's names in Mother Teresa's prayer, the names of those I had barely tol-erated for a long time. I began to recognize the poverty in them. Now I tease the Lord sometimes, saving, "I recognize you, Lord, in the disguise of John. I know you're there! You can't hide from me." It has become very easy.

I've also been praying for a spirit of compassion a lot since I am by nature very critical. Whenever I'm inclined to criticize a person, whenever I recognize their sin, their weakness, I be-gin to pray automatically, a little prayer from the Salesian Fa-thers, "A Prayer of Deep Sorrow," which begins, "Forgive me my sins, Lord, forgive, me my sins. . . ." It gives me a reflection of myself, where the Lord has taken me from, what he's done in my life, and enables me to be more compassionate toward others. I just continually pray, "Lord, forgive me my sins, my venial sins, my mortal sins."

This ability to pray continually has developed gradually over the years. Vatican II made me want to talk to God, but I felt restrained, thinking, "You don't talk to God; the prayers are all there. You can't approach God with your ordinary language, your mundane self."

After being blessed with the baptism in the Holy Spirit and coming into the charismatic renewal, I became very fluent in talking to God about everything. The baptism in the Holy Spirit brought me into awareness of God's personal love. As His child, I knew I had a right to crawl on His knees. I delighted in praising and thanking the Lord. It was like a curse was broken and a river opened.

I went along that way for some time, until a sort of dark night of the soul descended on me. God seemed absent. During this time, I went into the church one morning and said to the Lord, "I cannot bear this. I've walked in the light for so long, the darkness is totally untenable. I'll just sit here until you give me a word that will give me courage so I can go on for the rest of the day."

Nothing happened. I said, "Okay, I cannot tell you when to do what you will do, Lord. I can only ask, and I must go to work. So I will open the Scripture, and you will show me something, just a word for consolation." I opened to Psalm 63. Now it wasn't that I had not read that psalm before, but it became so soothing, "my soul thirsts for thee . . . as in a dry and weary land." I suddenly realized that David too experienced this longing for God. If that was good enough for David, a man after God's own heart, then I decided it was good enough for me, and I prayed along with him.

When God finally broke through that darkness, I had a much wider vision of God than I had ever had before. I thought I knew Him, but now I saw a new expanse of God. I was so happy. The darkness has come in many times since then, but every time I've known that at the end of the tunnel there would be a new and deeper revelation of God. Now I go through the darkness without panic, but with expectation.

For the most part these days, I find spontaneous, continuous prayer easy, so easy. I wake up with a prayer on my lips and in my heart. Whatever time in the night that I get up, there is something flowing, so I know that my spirit prays when I'm asleep. I'm in continuous prayer, and it flows from the heart. Lots of times I speak it aloud when I'm driving or doing my chores. Lots of times it just rolls in my heart without vocalization.

One way I pray continually is with ejaculations such as the Divine Mercy Chaplet, "For the sake of His sorrowful passion, have mercy on us and on the whole world." There is another one I've known since childhood: "Eternal Father, we offer you the precious wounds of your Son Jesus to heal the wounds of our souls. My Jesus, pardon and mercy through the merits of your sacred wounds." I find my heart is always crying out, "My Jesus, pardon and mercy," as I pray for the world.

Though I can say my prayer has changed from this to this to this over the years, I don't know how God will change it next. God is infinite, so I don't suppose we will ever come to the place where we could say, "I know God, and I know God, and I know God." I remember somebody saying to me once, "Oh, God wouldn't do that." I said, "You want to know something, I don't know what God will do. He can do anything. And He does the most amazing things. And He asks for the most unreal things."

So, even at age seventy-five, I don't know what God will do next. All I know is that when He is doing it, I want to be there, because it will be good!

Babsie Bleasdell, a popular conference speaker, is foundress of the Word of Life Prayer Community in Trinidad and Tobago.

6

With Difficulty

by Mike Aquilina

"I've come to believe that there are no failed efforts at prayer."

A few years ago, prayer was a fairly placid matter for me, a leisurely conversation I could usually carry on before the tabernacle of my parish church. That was when my wife and I had only one child, and before I got into the newspaper business.

I was just discovering some new depths in the truths of the faith, and it was my pleasure to talk them over with the Lord. It was kind of like a college bull session, only on Trinitarian life, the sacraments, and the nature of truth. My life had fewer details then, and I could give each one careful consideration in those quiet half-hours in St. Agatha's Church.

But how I pray now can be boiled down to a few words of description: I pray with difficulty, with effort, and only with help.

My wife and I have three children to care for these days. Besides our son, who is six, we now have two daughters, ages three and one.

My work has changed, too. Three years ago I took over editorship of the official newspaper of a lively diocese — six counties, two-hundred-twenty parishes, a rich Catholic culture, and a bishop who makes news almost daily. Like most Church organizations, we keep a small staff, but we work hard. Like all newspapers, we deal with the stress of daily deadlines, irate readers, personnel clashes, and rising paper costs. For many of these issues, the buck stops with me. I get through each busy day by "multi-tasking" — copy-editing on screen while I'm returning calls to public-relations people, opening mail while I plan next week's edition with the assistant editor. And my mind runs almost constantly in "pre-writing" mode, outlining the next op-ed piece or refining the questions I'll ask the curia cardinal tomorrow. I am haunted by an insatiable to-do list.

In all this I am like most working people today. As corporations "re-engineer" and "right-size" their "human resources," the workforce survivors fill their hours with far more duties. Everyone, it seems, is having trouble keeping pace. The relentless details follow us wherever we go. They follow me even to my prayer.

Though I still stop at St. Agatha's to pray before the tabernacle, I find that less and less of my attention falls to Jesus. I begin by speaking to Him from my heart, but within seconds I'm mentally copy-editing my editorial, drafting a memo, or wondering how I will ever resolve the latest complaint from one of my reporters.

These distractions come for a reason, I reason, and so I direct them to Jesus. "What would You have me do?" I try to be still to let Him respond, and to consider His example — in His own professional life as a craftsman, in His teaching, in His continuing life of humility among us in the Eucharist.

But before long, I'm trying to run on my own steam again. Then going back to Him.

Then turning back to me. And on and on I go.

My other daily devotions go pretty much the same way: starting the day with Mass (and trying not to plan my workday too much), praying the Rosary (Which decade am I on? What happened to the last two?), and reading the Scriptures (Have I been staring at the word "withered" for three minutes?).

When I compare my efforts at prayer today with the fascinations of three years ago, I sometimes feel that I'm failing. But with a moment's reflection, I know that this is not so. In fact, I've come to believe that there are no failed efforts at prayer.

I've come to believe that sometimes God wants us to see what we're capable of receiving, so He gives us great gifts — in insight, love, wisdom and communion. That's when He comes to us.

Other times, well, God wants us to see what we're incapable of, so He lets our petty distractions have their way. He says, "OK, now it's your turn: You come to Me."

Intermittently, in our prayer we come to see that we are made in God's image — we are made to think as He thinks, to love as He loves.

And then we come to see that we are worms, really, and not men (see Psalms 22:7).

There's an economy to this that keeps us from excessive pride, but keeps us from despair, too. What's important, I believe, is for me not to give in to the pride or the despair, to resist the urge to give up my times of prayer, simply because they don't feel very rewarding.

So I learn that I'm not very good at saying the Rosary after all. That's a beautiful thing. I'm a kid handing his mother the best "artwork" he can muster, an absurd concoction of construction paper, glue, and scribbles. And she loves it, and loves me all the more for it.

So I sometimes fall asleep on my knees in a darkened church. But there's a sure love in the struggle that led up to my dozing.

I think of my three-year-old, Mary Agnes, sitting on my lap at bedtime, struggling to stay awake and spend some time with me. She loses the battle, but wins my heart all the more.

My dozing and distractions teach me that I am a child like Mary Agnes — I am a son of God. That simple truth comes home to me more and more as my days grow ever more complicated. Not only is God mystery, power, glory, and majesty, but He is dear — even when I can't seem to tell Him the things that I should.

In these last few years, I have also come to appreciate the company of the saints, those friends who've "been there, done that," and now intercede for us before the Lord. Friendship never dies, even though our friends seem to leave us for awhile. Now, when the days get tough, I know the presence of my dear friend Bob, who died suddenly in 1989. I ask his advice and his prayers now, as I did when I could call him on the phone.

I've also come to count on St. Francis de Sales, the patron of my trade, who helps our staff make deadline each week. Especially, I've known the help and fatherly care of Blessed José Maria Escrivá de Balaguer, the founder of Opus Dei, the lay vocation to which God has called me.

But surely prayer isn't just for "prayer time." We're told to "pray without ceasing." So the struggle is pretty much constant.

Since I begin my day with a sleepy morning offering as soon as I roll out of bed, all the work that follows will rise to God as prayer — with or without my active consent at any given moment. Still, I try to "check in" whenever I can. In the press of the day, I try to key in on some signal — the ringing phone, for example — as my cue to tell my Father I love Him.

This workday awareness of His presence, though, doesn't come easily to me. And it doesn't come at all unless I stay faithful to my regular appointments in more formal prayer — my morning offering, the Mass, the Rosary, the Scriptures, and my conversation with God in mental prayer.

Spaced throughout the day, these prayers are like vines I

plant here and there along a wall. Pretty soon they reach out to cover more and more of my day.

For example, when I'm feeling worn out after three consecutive long days, I'm moved to pray in the words of the Mass: "This is my body, which will be given up for You." He understands that kind of sacrifice.

Or when I'm on my way to a politically charged meeting, the second Joyful Mystery of the Rosary will suddenly come back to me, and I'll ask Mary to help me to be as she was when she visited Elizabeth: to be a tabernacle of the peace of Christ.

I'm awed when I think that these little gifts all flow from what seem to be my failed attempts at prayer: a distracted Mass, a lost recitation of the Rosary.

I once read somewhere that there's no way of knowing what God is doing in one's own soul at any given moment. So what seems like great progress might be no great shakes, really. And what seems like failure. . . .

Well, in the end, there are no failed attempts at prayer, because it is the Holy Spirit who prays in us. It is God, perfect and all-powerful. And He cannot fail.

Even when I seem to be failing again and again.

Mike Aquilina, father of three small children, formerly was editor of The Pittsburgh Catholic, diocesan newspaper of the Diocese of Pittsburgh. He is now editor of New Covenant magazine.

7

Honestly

by Father Scott Seethaler, O.F.M. Cap.

"I asked God how to avoid being unfaithful. He told me to keep nothing from Him when I am praying."

At home, my parents made sure that I prayed at the prescribed times. In school, the nuns drilled me in my prayers. They taught me a word for remembering the four types of prayer: ACTS, which stands for adoration, contrition, thanksgiving, and supplication. Knowing how needy I was as a child, I considered supplication and contrition very useful prayers.

I grew up in a family that rarely used the word "love." I wasn't comfortable saying it to God. My strategy as a child was to placate God and avoid getting Him angry. I wanted to get to heaven, but not too quickly.

All this began to change in the eighth grade. I started to feel called to the priesthood. The young priest in my parish encouraged me to pursue my calling. I entered the seminary as a freshman in high school. Although we spent many hours in formal prayer, my energy was devoted to studies, sports, and trying to live with three hundred other frisky teenagers.

During those thirteen years in the seminary, I learned many things about myself. Chiefly, that I was a passionate man. It was very painful to watch my friends leave the seminary. Anger flared in me when I saw poverty, racism, and injustice. These intense emotions scared me until I started to read the psalms. I found all of my emotions in them. Since the psalms were inspired, I knew that God wanted me to bring my emotions to prayer. I am no longer embarrassed praying about my passions. When I am about to explode, I hear God say in Psalm 46: "Be still, and know that I am God."

The older I get, the more I appreciate the Bible. I'm amazed how much my life mirrors salvation history. Like the men of Scripture, I have had my moments of passionate fidelity. I also have had my moments of sinfulness and weakness like them. As I study Scripture, I see how people abused their power, wealth, and sexuality. In prayer, I have asked God how to avoid being unfaithful. He told me to keep nothing from Him when I am praying. I need to take all of my fears, temptations, and doubts to prayer. Praying is not always a pleasant experience when I am being completely honest. Yet the honesty keeps me connected to Jesus, Who invites me to intimacy with Him.

If you play with the word intimacy, it can be pronounced "into-me-see." I know that my prayer has to be transparent. Otherwise, I will be unfaithful. Intimacy with God doesn't happen all at once. In fact, it won't happen at all if we think that God is disgusted with our humanness. King David must have worried about this when he reminded God in Psalm 51 that he was conceived in guilt and sin. Original sin does make us slow to choose good. Yet God does not sit up in heaven clucking His tongue at our every mistake. He tells us that He is quick to forgive and will take us back with great tenderness.

One of my favorite prayers is to sit quietly and picture Jesus speaking to me. He says: "I love you, Scott, don't be afraid to come to me." Fear is the main obstacle to intimacy. Frequently in the Gospels Jesus speaks of fear. Reading the Gospels with regularity helps me to deal with my fears.

As a priest, I experience intimacy with Jesus in a unique way when I am praying the Mass. Some teenagers tell me that they get nothing out of Mass. I tell them that they get Jesus out of Mass. Perhaps that is why Christianity is really for adults. If you are serious about your faith, you have a hunger for intimacy. Children usually approach prayer as magic; adults as relationship. Like any relationship, intimacy with God goes through many phases. There are moments of joy, sorrow, euphoria, and monotony. One day I enjoy praying; the next it is a struggle.

I try not to worry about how I pray. The form I use depends on what is happening in my life. On days when life is difficult, my prayer is short and to the point. I simply keep saying, "Help!" God is pleased with this four-letter prayer. He loves to hear from us and delights in helping us. If all I can say is "Help," I keep the relationship alive.

Over the years, I have experienced many styles of praying. I think the style of praying is not as important as the fruits that flow from our prayer. Prayer is never an end in itself; it is a means to an end. I pray to stay a faithful and loving priest. When Jesus tells me in prayer that He loves me, my faith grows deeper. With this conviction, I am more willing to love as Jesus did. I believe that the acid test of a good prayer life is our capacity to love.

I'm celebrating my silver jubilee as a priest this year. The priesthood has changed during these twenty-five years. In recent years, it has received a great deal of bad publicity. The Church is experiencing a shortage of vocations. I realize that some priests have been unfaithful, yet the majority of us try to be good priests. Church history is filled with many saintly priests. Lately I have been praying for courage. It is desperately needed by priests today. We are called to live and preach the Gospels without compromise.

Many people have had their hope shaken because of all the pain in the world. I find myself preaching more about hope. It seems that the devil is tempting us to believe that God doesn't care and that prayer doesn't make a difference. Whenever my hope seems weak, I pray using chapter eight of Paul's letter to the Romans. It is filled with the conviction that God will help us conquer the evils in our world.

For seventeen years I have been a traveling preacher. With each passing year, I feel the need to pray more. My preaching is most authentic when I spend time in prayer before entering the pulpit. God sometimes surprises me when I preach. He gives me words that were not planned. With prayer, I feel the presence and power of God as I try to make the Gospels real for people.

Perhaps the biggest challenge to my priesthood is trying to help someone who has hit the "betrayal barrier." Sooner or later, we all hit it. It's when we pray for something and we don't get it. A loved one dies or is in great pain. You lose your job. A precious relationship is broken. Because of these experiences, we feel betrayed by God. Some people never recover from this sense of betrayal. They continue to live good lives but they have no enthusiasm for God or organized religion. They may go to church, but they cannot understand why God didn't answer their prayers. Many of these people have a deep sadness that won't go away. Despite their disappointment, I encourage them to pray because God will come with comfort and strength.

Currently, I am living with my mother. When she became sick, I decided to move into her apartment and take care of her. With each passing month she grows weaker. She is grieving the loss of her health. We pray together every day that God will bless her. There have been blessings, but it is hard for her to recognize them when she has so much pain. Sometimes she says to me, "God is not answering my prayer."

I try to comfort her by saying that God has sent me as the answer to her prayers. At night when she is sleeping in the next bed, I find myself saying to God that I need more faith to deal with all of my mother's health problems. I fight the feeling that God has abandoned us. Like the man in the Gospels, I say to Jesus: "I do believe; help my unbelief." I try to pray even when I don't feel like it.

As I pray, I hear God say that He wants me to take care of my mother. I remember hearing of an elderly priest who once said: "I used to get upset that my ministry was interrupted so often. Then I realized that the interruptions *were* my ministry." Taking care of my mother has interrupted my preaching ministry, but it has certainly taught me to be a warm, compassionate son. Now, when I do have a chance to preach, I see all the other caregivers in the congregation nodding their heads in agreement when I speak of the struggle to take care of our loved ones who are sick or elderly.

One biographer of St. Francis of Assisi said that there came a time in Francis' life when he was not so much praying as he was a living prayer. I would like this to happen in my life.

I think it happens when a person's prayer is filled with gratitude. Once we begin to count our blessings and say thank you, it will take up most of our time at prayer. Psalm 136 is a litany of thanksgiving. I often encourage people to write their own version of Psalm 136. It is a great remedy for people who are depressed or who wallow in self-pity. Gratitude leads to joy and happiness.

It is our prayer that helps us to act redeemed in good times and in bad. As long as we pray, we know the end of the story. God's plan may be temporarily frustrated by our abuse of free will, but in the end God will triumph. When I pray, I celebrate God's love as I wait for Jesus' final return.

Father Scott Seethaler, O.F.M. Cap., conducts a traveling preaching ministry based in Pittsburgh.

8

Late at Night

by Lou Jacquet

"Just one other thing, Lord. Bless this old house and protect it from further flood damage until we get that permanent sump pump installed, will You?"

How do you pray now?" I love being asked that question. It is so tempting to answer with something a bit flippant: "Desperately!" or "More than I thought I would need to" or "Obviously, not very effectively."

But I mean no irreverence. It is merely that, as the stepfather of six between the ages of seventeen and twenty-four, the last fourteen years of my life have been wrapped up in trying to help raise someone else's children with Gospel values. That can drive a man to prayer.

So while my first response might seem irreverent, my initial answers also contain a grain of truth. Prayer holds great peace for me on occasion. More often, however, it provides me with real hope on the days when I do not seem to be making any headway at all in the "Christian Stepfather of the Year" competition.

Let me acknowledge this at the start: I am not one of those people who has always found it easy to pray. I once interviewed a nun who told me that "prayer is as natural for me as breathing in and out." I never forgot her remark because it stands in rather marked contrast to my own history of prayer.

Unlike that nun, my prayer has been a series of peaks and valleys with more than a few years spent wandering in the desert. Which, I think, is not all bad. I know some believers whose prayer life is beautiful and simple and genuine. But I know plenty of others who struggle to pray. I don't think God loves us any less for the fact that we have to work hard at what comes naturally to others. In fact, when I interviewed Father John Shea and shared with him how much I wished I could recapture the enthusiasm in prayer that I had twenty-five years ago, he surprised me by saying that my struggles were a sign of maturation in prayer. That's good news for a lot of us.

Looking back, I can see how different my prayer is today from a decade or more ago. I am surprised, first of all, at how much more I pray now than I did then. The core of my prayer life is daily Mass, which I attend about three times a week. This is the single best thing I have ever done to improve my prayer. A day in which I spend half an hour with the Lord at Eucharist is qualitatively different from a day on which I do not. I can feel that in my bones. Sometimes, I pray in the car on the way to work, often for the persons whose paths I cross at stoplights. At other times, I find it helpful to pray over my appointment calendar, remembering specific intentions for those I will interview or meet with today.

Often I pray late at night when the house has quieted down. At such times, my wife is asleep and the three kids who still live

at home with us are either in for the night or out enjoying themselves for a final few minutes before curfew. I love that quiet
time. My number one prayer at such moments has been the
same since the kids became teenagers: "Lord, help them make
wise moral choices." I cannot be with them on dates, cannot be
everywhere to counteract the negative influences of this most
secular society we live in. But I can and do pray earnestly, often
with a sense of humor, asking God to watch over them.

Praying with Scripture late at night has also been rewarding. I turned to the psalms during personally difficult times a
decade ago and have found them to be both a marvelous source
of hope and a beautiful way to praise. At those times when
prayer seems especially difficult, I simply ask the Lord to accept my struggle to pray as heartfelt prayer in itself. Praying
that I might learn to pray better, with more conviction and be-
lief, seems itself a very fine form of prayer.

I realize that not everyone happens to be married to a spouse
like mine who plays piano and organ and sings for our parish
Masses. But since I have been blessed in that way, one of the
most rewarding ways in which I pray is at the piano, seated
next to my wife. Geri plays and sings, and I make an attempt to
sing along. Occasionally I simply listen and pray. Sometimes
our song is our prayer; sometimes we combine the words and
music with the Church's timeless Liturgy of the Hours or a
reading from Scripture. At such moments, my soul soars. There
is a great deal of truth in that old adage that "those who sing
pray twice." My prayer is never more fruitful than when Geri
plays and sings beside me at the piano. For persons without a
spouse to sing with at the piano, I'd recommend a tape of religious music as a background. Music taps into the sacred in a
special way.

Many folks, I know, have a set time of day to pray, but that
never seems to work for me. I have tried getting up early and
praying to begin the day, but not with great success. As a light
sleeper, I tend to fall asleep after 1 A.M. on a regular basis and
awaken a few hours later intent on survival rather than prayer.

So putting off praying until I'm out of the comatose stage, two or three cups of English Breakfast tea later into the morning, seems to work best for me.

A word about the Rosary. As a baby boomer who rejected it wholesale in the 1960s, I now heartily recommend this ancient form of prayer. I find it gives me great comfort at certain times to pray it. I use it as a mood setter to calm myself down, put my thoughts with Mary and Jesus and the saints, and begin to pray from the heart.

Posture for prayer is a matter of preference, of course. I pray while driving and often in a comfortable armchair at home, but now and then I feel compelled to assume the prone position which priesthood candidates take on their ordination day. I lie on the floor, face down, head on my arms, supported by a small pillow. It's a wonderful position for at least two reasons: It puts aside distractions and helps me focus on the prayer "moment" at hand, and it strikes me as a suitably humbling pose to approach the Almighty. Praying in this way reminds me that, for all my desire to be in charge of my life, a bit of humility in approaching God to ask or thank or praise is not without its merits.

Unlike a decade ago, when my prayer was either formulaic or tended toward angry prayers of supplication, my prayer today has developed a gentler edge. This is a direct result of becoming a quite different person following two personal crosses I encountered in 1988. The arrogance I had before those life-changing incidents has been replaced, by the grace of God, with a great deal more compassion than I ever exhibited before. That sense of brokenness shaped my prayer completely for a time and even now gives it scope and focus. I pray often, with special feeling and conviction, for the broken persons of my acquaintance.

I also tap frequently into the Church's "spiritual treasury," as the new *Catechism of the Catholic Church* refers to the Communion of Saints. I pray conversationally first to the well-known saints such as Monica — now there's a parent who persevered

— but I pray as well to Catholic mothers and fathers I have known who have gone before me in death, folks who genuinely lived out their beliefs on a daily basis. In tough situations as a stepparent or at work, when I cannot seem to see my way clear to a solution, I ask them to help me find patience, inner strength, and peace of heart. On countless occasions, they do.

When all else fails, I turn to my secret source of strength: two orders of contemplative women Religious pray for me, my work, and my family on a daily basis and have for years. Linking my prayers with theirs gives me a sense of deep peace. How can the Lord refuse what these selfless women ask for us?

It's late. My wife is asleep. I'm sitting in the old armchair in the corner of our bedroom, one leg swung over the side, talking to God about the day. "Watch over this household, Lord. Protect and guide Patrick, who has faced adversity and built a good life nonetheless. Help Tara, who's so much fun and so intense, to find a career that suits her talents. Help Rachel survive the day-to-day pressures of being a teenager and utilize all her marvelous talents in addition to her radar for finding teenage boys. Bless Geri as she sleeps. Bless Steve and Tony in faraway cities tonight; keep them free of the crippling addiction to drugs that robbed them of so much of their youth. Bless Jennifer as she prepares for marriage.

"Just one other thing, Lord. Bless this old house and protect it from further flood damage until we get that permanent sump pump installed, will You? I don't think I can face drying out the basement one more time. Remember why we are staying, Lord. The mortgage is paid off."

Lou Jacquet is editor of the Catholic Exponent, the newspaper of the Diocese of Youngstown, Ohio.

9

Letters to God

by Barbara Bartocci

"Writing forces my hand — literally. It strips away my veils of rationale; the comfortable lies I tell myself in order to deny the truth."

They stretch out on my bookshelf, a long line of them now . . . my prayer journals: those small, hardbound blank-page books you find in bookstores. In them, I write what I call my letters to God . . . to Father, Son, or Holy Spirit . . . and through my penned "correspondence" I process my fears, anxieties, doubts . . . and gratitude.

I pick them up at random, thumbing through pages from five years ago, or ten years ago, or last year on this very same day . . . and I see in my jottings both a testament to ways in which I have grown, and recognition of issues I still wrestle with.

An entry in May 1985: "O Lord, You are no stern, judgmental God from whom I must earn approval. You are Light and warmth, forever loving me. Your Light flows over, around and in me. . . . It is I who choose to walk into darkness, while You wait — patiently, lovingly — until I decide to return to the Light."

A decade later, I know it is still I who choose to leave the Light.

Writing to God goes beyond meditation or the murmur of spoken prayer; it gives me a wake-up call. It's a mirror of who I am and who I long to be, spelled out in the minutia of daily life. My journals help me see when I am replicating patterns — even if the people or situations have changed.

It's easy to live my life as if I'm driving down a familiar road, in a sort of autopilot trance, until suddenly, behind the steering wheel, I am startled back to consciousness, and I wonder, for one adrenaline-pulsed moment, "Where am I?" What wakes me on the road is the sudden braking of the car in front or a surprised realization, "That's my exit!" or the scary rush of a car that passes too close.

Yet how often do I work and play in a similar trance? Just going along so caught up in *daily busy-ness* that I stay asleep to deeper meaning or the ways in which small choices are building my life. Without a way to say "Halt!" I lose awareness of what is real.

Writing forces my hand — literally. It slows me down, pulls me over, wakes me up. It strips away my veils of rationale; the comfortable lies I tell myself in order to deny the truth, for inevitably the truth is this: I am not wounded or hurt or made whole by forces outside myself, but rather, by my own responses to life's events.

My journals remind me of the endless opportunities I have to co-create with God my personal universe through my free-will choices. I see my choices mirrored in my writing — the times I exploded in anger at my husband — or the self-pity I wallowed in when an editor turned down a story — or my envy of a friend who seemed to "have it all."

Yet, I see mirrored, also, my earnest *desire* to follow Christ's teachings, even though I often falter.

On March 25, 1988, I wrote: "O Lord, I am loathe to come before You this morning. My prayer feels hypocritical, for I have treated so harshly the very one in my life I claim to love most. Yet now, more than ever, I need Your love and spiritual guidance, and I thank You for accepting me as I am. Oh God, heed my cry for Your healing touch in my heart."

Even as I marvel that my higher desires are so frequently overrun by ego-driven behavior, I'm encouraged to realize how often I seek the higher road. Didn't Jesus promise, "Seek, and you will find" (Matthew 6:10)?

However, journals are not diaries — a dry compendium of each day's activities — so sometimes a week will pass in which I don't write at all; my prayers then revolve around reading and meditation. At other times, especially when I'm hurting, I may write copiously; my journals become an outpouring of passion or fear, anxiety or anger. And through the act of writing, it's as if God enters my heart to give me answers.

In April 1984, after my husband lost his business and was unemployed, I wrote: "I have struggled so this past week, torn in my emotions. Fear, anger, envy — all have gone to battle inside my soul. My deep desire to pursue a writing career is at war with the realities of my family situation. I have said many times, 'Thy will be done' (Matthew 6:10). Is Your will for me now to go to work and support my husband rather than to grow as a writer? It feels like a cross, but I must trust I have not been given a talent only to live in pain because pursuing it stays out of reach."

A year later, in another, less stressful time, I wrote: "Thoughts while sitting in the steam room at the gym: God has created so many different bodies; so many different souls. The sheer wonder of it all! Yet our similarities far exceed our differences. Give me the wisdom to honor differences and celebrate likenesses, O Lord."

Occasionally, my correspondence with God brings immediate response. With my non-dominant writing hand (since I'm left-handed, that means my right hand), I'll let words flow onto paper from my subconscious. In scraggly printing, like a first grader's, I reread an entry from March 1990 which says, "Barbara, be not afraid, I am with you always and All Ways. You are My child and much loved." The message still comforts me.

Sometimes, answers appear through the dreams I record (in Scripture, don't dreams act as conduits from God?). Sometimes, I find comfort in quoting others. At a time when I struggled with another career disappointment, I quoted Pope John XXIII, who wrote in his own "Journal of a Soul":

"It is hard for me to think of a hidden life, neglected, perhaps despised by all, known to God alone; yet until I succeed in doing such violence to my own likes and dislikes that this obscurity becomes not only indifferent but welcome and enjoyable, I shall never do what God wants from me."

I felt encouraged to realize that Pope John, too, had had a career disappointment. As an old man, he convened Vatican II and opened the windows of the Catholic Church. How do I know at what age God can best use me?

When I write my letters to God, I can review, process, and find a more loving, positive way to handle the struggles in life. Writing helps me leave behind my ego state (if only momentarily) and move to higher ground. I learn to *see* differently; and years later, as I reread my penned tears and joy, insights and growth, I find, in my letters, what a hand God has had in my life.

Barbara Bartocci, author of Unexpected Answers *and many other books, lives in Shawnee Mission, Kansas.*

10

Beads and Mysteries

by Father Richard Antall

"The Rosary gives a kind of narrative line for my life — from grace and call, to the cross and suffering and then to the hope of glory. It is a package I feel the need to go over every day."

Sometimes I wonder when I see a Catholic in the casket whether the Rosary wrapped about his hands really meant anything to him. I have joked that some people ought to have the remote control in their hands instead of the Rosary. If somebody places the beads in my cold hands after this life is over, however, it will not be just a badge of Catholicism, because the

Rosary is an integral part of my life. However, it hasn't always been this way.

When I was in seminary, we never once said the Rosary in common. The very few of the students who did pray it were considered relics of bygone times. That was during the *Sturm und Drang* days of the '70s, when nearly everybody was a little crazy.

I remember my brothers and sisters gave me a nice Rosary once for a birthday, figuring that it was something a seminarian would be happy to have. At the time, I would rather have had one of those books of the hour by some theologian. My prayer was too pretentious for the Rosary.

Only after I was ordained a priest did I begin to say the Rosary with more regularity. I think this was a result of living in a parish and appreciating the devotion of the people who said the Rosary after daily Mass. Today canon law says that seminaries ought to foment the Rosary and other Marian devotions, but in those days I could see that seminary spirituality was very different from what one saw in the parish.

I began a daily Rosary for my mother soon after my father died. His death came just five weeks after I was ordained a priest. He couldn't come to my ordination, although I did offer Mass at home. Near the end of his short battle with cancer, he had been able to receive only the Precious Blood.

The Rosary I said, and still say, for my mother was with the Glorious Mysteries. I suppose at first my intention was like what the poet says in "A Sonnet To My Mother," "may she go from mourning to morning," but now I take it as seriously as I do the Divine Office. It is something concrete I do to put me in touch with my mother in prayer, no matter where I am in the world.

When a good friend was leaving the priestly ministry, I decided to pray another Rosary each day for him. He was in a crisis that he thought was celibacy-related. Sadly, he discovered it was something else, but it was too late. I had said the Sorrowful Mysteries for him because I thought of his anguish and the pain of the Church.

He left the ministry, but I kept saying the Rosary for priests. During the depressing time of the scandals about priests, made worse by the anti-Catholic animus behind some of the reporting, the Sorrowful Mysteries were my way of coping. Christ suffered the agony of realizing He carried the ugliness of all our sins, the sins of the whole world. All sinfulness pressed into the chalice of suffering He had to take up. No wonder He sweat blood!

I said two parts of the Rosary every day. This was a good deal for someone who two years before would have had to look for the Rosary beads. I suppose it was inevitable that I join the Joyful Mysteries to the Sorrowful and the Glorious.

There are so many intentions that priests are aware of. People constantly ask for our prayers, or we are aware of their need for them. The poor, the sick, the hardened sinners, the confused, all cross our paths and we need to pray for them. So I added another Rosary each day. When I pray the Joyful Mysteries, I pray for whatever parish I am serving.

The complete Rosary is like a Cook's tour of salvation, from the Annunciation, in which we see the God who fulfills His promises of salvation, to that promise worked out for the mother of Jesus in her coronation in heaven; we see the history of the world and can reflect on our own history. We have been asked to believe like Mary; we have also been promised a crown after the cross of this life.

There are some days when all my meditation is the Mysteries of the Rosary. I march through the Mysteries, associating my life with Jesus' life and remembering people in trouble. The Rosary gives a kind of narrative line for my life. The thread goes from grace and call (the Joyful Mysteries) to the cross and suffering and then to the hope of glory. It is a package I feel the need to go over every day.

I associate petitions with Mysteries. Some of them are due to events in my life and others are long-standing. Every time I pray the Mystery of the descent of the Holy Spirit at Pentecost,

I remember to ask for the gift to preach well in Spanish. The petition occurred to me when I was in mission school, and I have never stopped asking for that particular bit of the grace of Pentecost in my life.

When I was in formation, the Rosary was looked down upon as something for mere beginners in prayer. It had served its purpose when the illiterate were imitating the psalter of the monks, but it was passé. Prayer with the open Bible was the ideal. Or centering prayer or *poustinia* or prayer partners or icons. Everyone was going to be the next St. Teresa of Ávila or St. John of the Cross.

I am still far from the grace of infused contemplation. I am embarrassed to say that my attempts at making myself the fabled contemplative in the world of action have not succeeded. As I get older, I feel more in common with those illiterate peasants for whom the Rosary was a lifeline of prayer. The Rosary for me is like my morning constitutional of the spirit, a walk along the way of salvation.

What has held me together has been a sense of communion with Jesus through Mary. The Rosary helped me as a young priest in a bluc-collar suburb of Cleveland, and then as a missionary in El Salvador. It was a consolation when I served as a campus minister and now it is both a challenge and comfort.

Every day I meditate on Christ's saving work and become more aware of the fragility of my own life and work. The narrative line helps me with perspective.

At forty-one, my age makes me aware of thc cycles of life. Experience had taught me to respect problems because they often return in some way. I started saying the Rosary for my mother because of her grief for my father. Thirteen years after the death of my father, my mother remarried and I continued to pray the Glorious Mysteries for her. She had the consolation of someone close to her, someone very good to her. God was sharing His favors with her. Then grief entered once more, when my stepfather died. Still, I am praying the Glorious Mysteries for my mother in this fresh sadness.

Although I did not say the Rosary at the time I first sensed my vocation, it is what I recommend to anyone thinking of serving the Lord in priesthood or religious life. (That, and the reading of the Scriptures on a daily basis in order to read the whole Bible.) I do not know how I did without the Rosary as long as I did.

I read that the Holy Father says the Rosary before all his other prayers. Many times I have been calmed for prayer by first reaching for my beads. The Rosary, with its meditations, helps me prepare for Mass, or difficult encounters. It accompanies me in the confessional and on walks. My poor sense of prayer is fortified by the telling of the beads. I would be lost without it.

Anyone who writes of prayer should either be a saint or acknowledge his or her unworthiness. In a year's time, I hope that my essay about prayer would reflect improvement in reverence, diligence, and inspiration. However, what I know for certain is that the Rosary will always be a part of my prayer life. The cycles of my life, my intentions, and my aspirations will echo the Mysteries I meditate day by day.

If it is not a part of your prayer, I recommend it to you. If it is, be glad for this late starter who has received so much through the prayer of the mother of Jesus.

"Pray for us, O holy Mother of God
"That we be made worthy of the promises of Christ."

Father Richard Antall is pastor of St. Mary's Church in Painesville, Ohio.

11

Without Ceasing

by Joe Pisani

*"Four years ago, prayer was nothing more to me
than two minutes a day giving directions to God,
if I could squeeze Him into my crowded
schedule."*

E very morning at 4:55, my clock radio **wakes**
me with the unsettling news of another day: **blood**
shed in Bosnia, random slayings on the **streets of**
New York, political scandals, traffic jams **on the**
highway, and, of course, the weather — **cloudy**
with showers.

After five minutes of this seemingly interminable **litany of**
crisis and catastrophe, I've listened to enough bad news **to know**
nothing changed overnight in the real world, so I turn **off the**

radio and roll out of bed to begin my sojourn in a far more hospitable environment — the spiritual world.

Still somewhat bleary-eyed, I start my ninety-minute morning regimen of prayer and meditation in the quiet solitude of my living room.

Let me confess: Four years ago, prayer was nothing more to me than two minutes a day giving directions to God (if I could squeeze Him into my crowded schedule). I was sure an omniscient Deity understood my predicament: the excessive demands of my personal and professional life, especially with a career in journalism. I didn't ignore God, but my prayers were nothing more than delegating to Him the problems I couldn't deal with because I was too preoccupied with breaking news and deadlines.

"God, my daughter is having trouble with algebra, and I don't have time to tutor her. Would you handle that situation, please?

"While you're at it, God, make sure I have enough money in my checking account to pay the mortgage.

"Oh, and God, it would help if You put in a good word with my boss because I really need that promotion."

And so it went, day after day, year after year, until suddenly and inexplicably, with no prior warning, my life changed. Somewhere, somehow, someone must have been praying for me because I experienced a conversion after reading an item on the Associated Press wire about a little-known village called Medjugorje, where the Blessed Mother was believed to be appearing to six children. Now, this was a news story!

In the weeks that followed, I asked Our Lady for some spiritual CPR for my soul, and she wasted no time in responding. I still don't fully understand what happened, nor do my family members and friends.

My mother thinks I've become a fanatic — a regular fool for Christ, you might say. My teenage daughters merely sigh and roll their eyes. My wife is convinced I missed my true vocation as a Benedictine. And my intimate coworkers claim it's a mid-life crisis. I, on the other hand, have a simpler explanation: it's the power of the Holy Spirit.

Since that momentous occasion, I've learned a few valuable lessons:

• Prayer is listening more than it is talking. Once I took the cotton out of my ears and stuffed it in my mouth, my prayer life improved dramatically.

• The Holy Spirit is, quite simply, addictive, which means to say, the more you pray, the more you want to pray. At one time, I couldn't sit through the Rosary even if my soul depended on it, but now I can appreciate all forms of prayer.

• Prayer has become the most important activity in my life; it's like spiritual breathing. Without it, the soul dies.

• You need quiet time alone with God every day.

Rising at 4:55 A.M. is the only way I can avoid interruptions from my four daughters, one wife, two goldfish, and one hamster. I've discovered this is the best time to pray, largely because God can speak to me through my thoughts early in the morning.

Every morning, I walk downstairs to the dark living room, light a vigil candle, invoke the Holy Spirit, and begin with a half-hour of centering prayer. I relax and try to put myself in the presence of the Lord so I can experience Him personally in the depths of my being.

While sitting in the quiet, dark room, I listen for the still, small voice of God, which isn't as easy to do as it might seem, because my mind has a tendency to preview the upcoming day's events, along with the confrontations and crises that await me.

When I finish meditating, I pray the Joyful Decades of the Rosary and the Liturgy of the Hours, followed by several litanies and prayers for the souls in purgatory, the pope, the Church, and the unborn.

This tranquillity is short-lived and ends abruptly when my fifteen-year-old daughter bounds out of bed and starts getting ready for school to the accompaniment of slamming closet doors, running water, and a high-powered blow-dryer.

No matter, it's time to leave for seven o'clock Mass, and I drive to join a dozen or so people in a Polish church run by the Vincentians. For twenty years, I was a lapsed Catholic who didn't attend Mass on Sunday, much less during the week, but now daily Mass is central to my spiritual life.

After Mass, I rush to catch the 8:04 train. During my drive to the station, I pray the Sorrowful Mysteries of the Rosary. During my morning commute, I say various novenas and pray for family members and friends, living and dead.

More importantly, I pray for complete strangers I've only read about. Their names appear in crime stories in the tabloid newspapers and their pictures are on the evening news — they are murderers and molesters, child abusers and celebrities, terrorists and serial killers. Increasingly, I've come to realize the need to pray for these pathetic souls. After all, isn't that what Christ wanted? Even though I sometimes think my feeble appeals for their conversion and salvation are futile, I've learned never to underestimate the power of prayer, supercharged by God's grace. I've also learned that if I concentrate on praying for the needs of others, God will take care of my needs.

Throughout the workday, I offer up prayers for strangers I meet — the taxi driver, the train conductor, the chronically disgruntled man at the newsstand, and the sullen waitress at the diner. I'm convinced such anonymous and unsolicited prayers by some saint in disguise led to my conversion.

Even during the busiest time of day, I look for occasions to pray — at the much-dreaded meeting to discuss database marketing, while standing in the long line at the supermarket, or while sitting in the crowded Japanese restaurant waiting for sushi. A few precious moments are all it takes to invoke the Holy Spirit, to utter the Jesus Prayer, to ask my guardian angel for help, or to solicit the comforting love of the Blessed Mother.

Never say you don't have enough time for prayer. If you ask the Holy Spirit to help arrange your daily calendar, you'll be surprised at the results and discover that praying without ceasing isn't as impossible as it sounds. Moreover, you'll realize the power of prayer in your day-to-day struggles. I often call on Christ to defuse an embarrassing situation in the newsroom or ask the Holy Spirit to inspire me when I confront what seems to be an unsolvable problem.

Three times a week, I skip lunch and go to the gym, where I jog one hundred eight laps (four miles) around the indoor track. It's pure mind-numbing monotony in the cause of physical fitness, and my friends have asked, "Why the heck do you spend so much time running in circles? Doesn't it drive you crazy?" At one time it did, and in my past life, I would daydream about my 401(k) investments or brood over problems at home. Now, I use that time more productively in prayer, developing body and soul.

After jogging, I do eighty sit-ups, which I offer to the Sacred Heart of Jesus and the Immaculate Heart of Mary. Making such small sacrifices is a form of prayer we routinely neglect but one that has tremendous potential. Many years ago, the nuns taught me the importance of "offering it up," and their advice still holds true.

In the afternoon, if time permits, I'll walk across the street to St. Mary's Church, sit in front of the tabernacle, and give Jesus a progress report on my day. A few minutes in quiet conversation with Christ nourishes my soul. He's my best friend, and He's a good listener. He always has an answer or an encouraging word, which He'll place in my heart. Praying without ceasing, I've come to realize, means having a constant interior dialogue with Jesus.

On the train ride home, I read the Bible, starting by asking the Holy Spirit to enlighten me so I'll see the deeper meaning, which in my haste and obtuseness I might otherwise overlook. Later, I pray the Glorious Mysteries of the Rosary and pray in tongues, which I once swore I would never, ever, not in a million years, do. (It was too other-worldly, too weird.) My attitude, however, changed several months ago after I attended a Life in the Spirit retreat and decided to give it a try. What better way to spend time alone in the car? It sure beats listening to the top forty tunes on the radio. Finally, I'll get in some spiritual reading before bedtime and pray the Chaplet of Divine Mercy.

Despite this daily regimen of prayer, my teenage daughters often remind me I'm no candidate for sainthood, and my wife's frequent and humbling observation is, "How can a guy who prays so much be so short-tempered?" To which I can only respond: "Imagine what I'd be like if I didn't pray."

The truths I've learned are simple ones: prayer works; all prayer is good; all prayer is answered. The changes may be imperceptible at first, because the human eye is unaccustomed to detecting spiritual progress. Nevertheless, weeks, months, and years later, I believe I'll plainly see the dramatic results, and be overwhelmed to realize how much God has graced my feeble efforts.

Joe Pisani edits a daily newspaper in Connecticut. He also writes "One Man's Opinion," a column for Our Sunday Visitor, a weekly Catholic newspaper.

12

As an Adult Woman

by Catherine Fournier

"God had me on an endurance test. Not to see how much I could take, but how much I couldn't take."

I remember clearly the concern in the women's voice. "What are you doing, little girl?" She had come out to get the Saturday morning paper just as I was passing, wearing my headdress of brilliant purple thistles and singing to myself. It was 6:30 on a fresh, beautiful summer morning and I was barely six.

"Just exploring," I told her cheerfully.

"Does your mommy know you're out?" she asked, still looking very worried. I wondered why.

"Oh, no," I replied, "everyone is asleep, so I just go quietly." Did she guess that I was praying, that for children this is prayer?

A few years later, I found a special place, a clump of birch trees growing around a big rock. It seemed made just for me. Sometimes when I went there, the sight of those slim, white trees or sunlight on the mossy rock would make me breathless with excitement. I was overwhelmed by the beauty of the place, the sense that nature was so much bigger than me.

In my teens, I joined a young naturalists' club. We went on field trips every weekend, collecting plants, rocks, and wet feet. In the company of intelligent young people with similar interests, I relearned what I'd always known, that nature was infinitely varied, grand, and delicate, both unchanging and always changing.

It was a secular understanding of nature, though. I had little use for God, mostly because I thought He had little use for me. Sporadic church attendance had taught me to believe in God and the existence of heaven and hell; I'd just never seen any evidence of His interest in my life. My parents' marital difficulties, several moves, and the resulting social problems at school convinced me that I had to look after myself; no one else would.

In my late teens, I left home for college and "the real world." Like many young people who experiment with new ideas, I created a new identity, putting aside what I thought were childish things. Though it hurt, I replaced my love of nature and optimistic attitude with a preference for the realities of science and a cynical view of the workings of the world. I suppressed emotion as unreliable and followed intellect.

With a few notable exceptions. Even though I would have scoffed at the idea as unprovable and immeasurable, God *was* taking an interest in my life. Through an apparent "accident" of timing, God placed a good man — honest, loving, and honorable — right in the middle of the sterile, safe road I had charted for my life. "When you find the perfect spouse," I told myself, "it's reasonable to marry him even if you're only eighteen."

My husband is Catholic. Soon after our marriage I converted. This was an another departure from rationality, especially to my lukewarm Presbyterian parents. What they didn't know was that I had been searching since my early teens for a spiritual home, for some answers and certainty to questions that haunted me. Why was I born? What was I supposed to be doing? Why had God made the world?

While I still thought of God as distant and uninvolved, like the constellation of Orion or Ursa Major, my conversion answered many questions. I learned that God had made the world (and me) for a specific purpose, and that the Catholic Church is historically and doctrinally intact from the time of Christ. These were good, sound, rational arguments for conversion. I learned that I should pray to know God and His will.

I had never learned to pray, and was faced with a new set of questions. Could I ask for things, or should I only praise Him? Did I have to pray out loud? Should I use prayers I found in a book?

So, carefully and methodically, like a scientist, I began learning about prayer. I read, I prayed at specific times, I searched with all my energy and determination for the sense of peace and certainty I saw in other Catholics. Many times I stopped in frustration for days or months, sure that I wasn't getting anywhere or doing it right.

Yet, like hearing voices on the breeze when you're looking for someone, every once in a while I'd catch an echo of what I was seeking. A sudden sense of homecoming, the comforting weight of a loved one's hand on your shoulder, one time a vision of sitting on Mary's lap weeping with joy. Innumerable times, God reassured me that He was still there, still waiting, just enough to convince me to try again.

My father had just been diagnosed with cancer when our fourth child, Matthew, was born. My grandmother had died the day before his birth. The house we were renting was unexpectedly sold and we had to find new accommodations. Peter was in danger of losing his job, and our second and third children (a boy and a girl) were uncontrollably hyperactive. I remember sobbing in the confessional that I felt like God had me on an endurance test.

Still, the afternoon I came home with Matthew, I was flooded with a feeling of utter happiness. "Everything's going to be all right," I heard. "Don't worry." I lay on the couch, my baby cradled in my arm, the other children nestled around me, and wondered what I had done to achieve this feeling, what trick of the mind or prayer I finally had learned?

A question like that reveals I hadn't learned anything, of course. I continued to chase God with prayer for several years. Until, finally, I gave up. I was so tired of looking for God, so tired of trying to do everything, be everything, so afraid of never reaching God, that I quit. "I can't do this anymore, God," I said out loud one day. "If You want me, You're going to have to come and get me."

I don't know what I expected; I didn't really care anymore. There were no choirs of angels, no sudden transformation of my personality, no miracles. But I began to worry less, to be happy as a permanent condition rather than a fleeting moment. I forgave an old deep wound. I trusted my husband with my secret fears. I started to see God's hand in the course of my family's life and I trusted Him, too.

Rather than finding God, or God finally coming to me, I realized that he'd been there all along. I guess that's what's called a spiritual conversion, a good dozen years after my intellectual conversion.

Not a wasted dozen years, not by any means. I could not have accepted a spiritual conversion without an intellectual one first, nor would I have recognized it for what it was without the years of struggle in between. I needed to learn the structure and habit of prayer to God before I was ready to learn the freedom and spontaneity of prayer with God.

I was right — God had me on an endurance test. Not to see how much I could take, but how much I couldn't take. God waited until I was past my endurance, then He picked me up. Babies are carried, two-year-olds struggle to be put down to walk on their own, and seven-year-olds are too proud to be carried. By the time we're adults, we've forgotten all about being carried and being childlike, so God teaches us again.

How do I pray now?

I pray as I did as a child, knowing now that the infinite variety and beauty that enthralled me as a child is a reflection of God, His wisdom, mercy, and love for us. Every day, snowflakes, a hilltop of trees, sunsets and sunrises, even dandelions, inspire prayers of thanksgiving, often wordless, sometimes (to my children's horror) sung.

I pray as I did as a new convert, with the Mass, morning and evening prayers, the observance of feast days, and devotions, not with fear that God will reject me if I do it wrong, but with gladness. I pray knowing now that God created His Church and its rituals for His children, as parents create routines to guide and discipline their family.

I pray as a wife and mother, loving and serving God through my family, knowing now that their soft cheeks and sleepy breath are gifts from God. If the wonderful intricacies of a leaf are a reflection of God's splendor, how much more splendid is God's creation of a child! I pray with hugs and cookies, with the Rosary and special intentions, with seeing into their hearts and praying for their futures.

I pray as an adult woman, both silently and out loud, knowing now that how I pray is not as important as the fact that I do pray. I pray throughout the day knowing now that when I pray is not as important as remembering that who I pray to is always listening.

Catherine Fournier writes from Arnprior, Ontario, where she and her husband, Peter, are raising six children. She is assistant editor for Nazareth Journal.

13

My Anchor

by Christopher Bell

"The closer I can remain to the Office, the better state I am in."

O*Lord, help me. As I attempt to write how You, You who are all powerful, all mighty, all loving, forgiving, merciful, have allowed me to speak with You, listen to You, fall away, and return to You. You allow me to live and breathe and know You. This, all this, is so marvelous and beyond my understanding. From before I was born, You knew me and all my ways. You know what is in my mind even before I can think of it.*

Lord, why You allowed me, from my earliest days, to know that You are, I cannot begin to explain. How can I repay You, for all your goodness to me? I want to say with the psalmist, "I will lift up the cup of salvation and call on the name of the Lord."

By the time I was in first grade, I knew Our Lord as I knew my parents. God existed as real as anyone. What happened in that year was my coming to know that Jesus, whose cross was in the front of the room, died for me and the whole world and no one, no athlete, no singer, no superstar, could ever be worth emulating more than Him. I knew I wanted to be like Him. How far away from Him I have gone. How sorry I am for denying Him. Yet, I look at St. Peter and have hope.

My prayer as a child certainly was childlike. I remember Mass in Latin and still know many of the responses. When I was told Jesus was in the white host, I was sure I could see Our Lord's face when the priest held up the host. I knew our nearly one-hundred-year-old, white wooden church was God's house, and could smell it in the incense and burning candles.

As I grew older, I always knew I wanted to remain close to Our Lord and try to be more like Him. But I am not a heroic type and don't even have the sense to know the right moral road to take. I came to know St. Augustine's misguided prayer long before I ever heard of any Doctor of the Church: "Lord make me good, but not yet." I thought I was good, basically, that is. Yet I had to find my own way, not bother God with such problems as I ran into. Besides, Our Lord ascended into heaven and left us with the Holy Spirit to do the best we can with what we have.

My conversations with God, during walks, at Mass, before confession, were one-way. I said what was on my mind and proposed a solution. When the words sounded appropriate for my taste, I followed my own advice, sometimes.

During college, I thought I needed to find my own way, completely. As Cardinal John Henry Newman wrote:

I loved to choose and see my path; but now
Lead thou me on.
I loved the garish day, and,

spite of fear,
pride ruled my will: remember
not past years.

While I was following my own way and not going to Mass often, I still had an inner urge — truly it must have been from God — to at least say the Lord's Prayer. I would say it almost daily, in the car, on my way to work. A simple Our Father. I know now that small prayer kept me from doing worse.

Eventually, however, I realized how sinful my ways had become. I had strayed far, far away from Our Lord. Even though I had returned to regular Mass attendance, I hadn't been to confession. I was receiving Our Lord in the holy, Blessed Sacrament. I prayed very hard now with the priest, "Let this (the Blessed Sacrament) not bring me condemnation, but health in mind and body."

How wonderful and beautiful is God to reach down and let me see again, in a clearer light, that now I needed Him. At this moment, I needed His cross, I needed His death and resurrection to forgive me, personally. This great epiphany opened my poor eyes to the sorry state of my soul. I not only needed Our Lord and His forgiveness and mercy, I needed His Church. I went to confession, and perhaps for the first time in my life, I knew I needed Jesus Christ to save me.

All this led me to Covenant House in New York, and its ministry to troubled and homeless youths. There I began not only a five-year stay in the lay, prayer community, but I found a new vocation working in and for the Lord. Working for the Lord requires constant prayer.

The greatest discovery in the prayer community was the Liturgy of the Hours, commonly called the Office or the Breviary. These wonderful psalms, canticles and hymns, readings, intercessions, responses, including the Lord's Prayer, laid out for each hour of the day, each day of the liturgical year, for each divine season, help me focus on the Lord's call to make this day holy, and, even more importantly, to listen to His call in what makes this day holy: what mystery in His angels and saints, in His foster father and Blessed Mother, in His Son and Spirit, in Himself is being revealed today, for me. How wonderful and grateful I am to know and be able to pray the Liturgy of the Hours.

> I cry with my voice to the LORD
>> with my voice I make supplication to the LORD,
> I pour out my complaint before him,
>> I tell my trouble before him.
> When my spirit is faint,
>> thou knowest my way!"
>
> *Psalm 142*

When I decided I was going to leave the prayer community in 1984, I feared that I would not have the support and structure I needed to continue to pray the Office daily. That is still a real fear.

When St. Francis Home, our first home for single mothers and children, now under the sponsorship of Good Counsel, Inc., opened in Hoboken, New Jersey, in March 1985, I was so busy that I was barely able to get to daily Mass, much less pray the Office.

My wise and prudent spiritual director and friend, Father Benedict Groeschel, urged me to return to daily Morning Prayer and Evening Prayer. As soon as I returned, balance was restored in my life. Not just my prayer life, my entire life.

The closer I can remain to the Office, the better state I am in. Daily Mass and frequent confession are a must. The Office, like part of a serious exercise regimen, fills out the entire program.

My wife, Joan, a devout Catholic with a Franciscan spirit, loves the Rosary along with the Divine Office, and challenges me in carrying out my prayers into my daily living.

Today, almost four years into marriage, as parents of one child and numerous kids in and out of our care almost from the beginning, our prayer life is still a challenge. No routine exists. But daily Mass, attempts at frequent confession, greater attempts at praying the Office, and daily Rosary are always in the mix of trying to stay spiritually healthy.

At the end of a long day, when all is said and done, if the kids are awake enough, we will end with an Act of Contrition, Angel of God, several petitions, and a deep sigh: Thank You, God, for the close of another day.

I enjoy, more than anything I've ever said or done, to hear my daughter repeat, first thing in the morning, "Thank You God for a new day."

Then, we begin again.

Christopher Bell is founder and director of Good Counsel in Hoboken, New Jersey, a home for unwed mothers and their children.

14

A Wildflower

by Bishop Joseph McKinney

"I could usually point to some activity every day that I thought pleased God. Now I saw that my activity does not make me beautiful; God *makes me beautiful."*

One day, while walking in early spring in a remote part of the woods, I stopped to pick a wildflower. As I gazed at its delicate beauty, a quiet awe filled my soul. I found myself saying, "You are so beautiful and yet nobody would have appreciated you if I did not notice you." As I dropped the flower, a thought crossed my mind, "You never stopped to admire a flower before and certainly never talked to a flower." Still, that quiet awe continued to bring a delicate joy to my being. I found myself humming a tune.

Some weeks later, I was involved in a time of reflective prayer. I asked the question, "Lord, when were You trying to speak to me this past month?" I reviewed my calendar and reflected on the many ways God had touched me. I listed forty items. None of them struck me as the key moment.

Then I remembered the moment with the flower. The Lord spoke, "That quiet awe was Me. I was trying to tell you! It's all right to be a flower in the woods."

I am a bishop. I have a full schedule of activities — work for the Church, for the Lord. I was not accustomed to thinking of myself as a flower in the woods. I seldom regard myself as one of His masterpieces. To the contrary, I acted as if I had to earn God's love.

Now, like sunshine breaking through the clouds, God's light broke into the shadows of my spiritual blindness. I realized that God is pleased with me just the way I am because He loves all His creations, especially humans. We have the glory of reflecting His image and likeness. Before that moment, I could usually point to some activity every day that I thought pleased God. Now I saw that my activity does not make me beautiful; *God* makes me beautiful. This made a colossal difference in my life — including my prayer life.

Reflective moments like that are common to my life now. I try to pray this way at least twenty minutes each day. For the past nine years I have kept a daily record of my reflections.

I believe the disciples on the road to Emmaus offer a profound model of prayer. Their hearts were burning within them because they were with the risen Lord. We all have the same opportunity daily if we take the time to be with Him.

My introduction to reflective prayer came ten years ago in a time of great stress. I had burned out, and had to resign my position until I was restored to health of mind and body. I went to a retreat house run by my friend Monsignor David Rosage. He offered some sage advice. "Relax, relax, relax," he said. "You are like most people who come here. You don't know how to relax. Some people like to lie on the beach and soak in the sun. Why don't you just get comfortable and soak in God's love?"

That led to twenty minutes of reflective prayer each day. It's part of my survival kit. When I pray the breviary or read Scripture each day, I make a special effort to note the whisperings of the Holy Spirit deep within me. As soon as some word causes a simple vibration in my heart, I spend twenty minutes relaxing with the Lord and soaking in its meaning. Usually it's a single word.

Today it was the word "send." "As the Father has sent me, even so I send you" (John 20:21). Thoughts started to flow. Jesus is always identifying Himself as being sent. He knows that he's here to reveal God's point of view and announce the Good News of salvation. He's constantly seeking the Father's will because He is sent. He is an ambassador of the Holy Trinity. He and the Father send us the Holy Spirit so we can be ambassadors for the kingdom of God. The Holy Spirit reveals God's will and empowers the disciples to go forth and spread the Good News. I, too, am sent. It's part of my identity. God gave me His Holy Spirit so that the urge to spread the Good News is ever-present. I'm an ambassador for God's kingdom. That's a great honor, and I want to accept it. I'm an ambassador because I'm sent. God can even use *me!*

That prayer was not only relaxing and invigorating, but it also helped me set priorities for the day. Going forth in the name of the Lord has new meaning.

When people come to me with depression or are overburdened by the struggles of life, I ask them, "How do you pray?" Reflective prayer is the best way I know to live the truth. "Come to me, all who labor and are heavy laden, and I will give you rest" (Matthew 11:28).

Reflective prayer grows significantly out of my personal devotion to the Holy Spirit.

When I understood that Jesus was led by the Holy Spirit, I wondered how that happened. I asked deeper questions about how I relate to the Holy Spirit. We are taught that the Holy

Spirit is a person. That calls for interaction. To ignore a person or give them the silent treatment is to be arrogant.

Jesus taught that the Holy Spirit is Paraclete: the person we call on to be at our side. "Come, Holy Spirit" is an appropriate way to relate to the Holy Spirit. What if the Holy Spirit comes? Then what?

To be led by the Holy Spirit, one has to learn how to hear the Holy Spirit. The Holy Spirit whispers and inspires. One has to be quiet and in a listening posture to hear the Holy Spirit.

I started my efforts at reflective prayer by taking three minutes at the end of each day and asking the question, "Did you try to lead me today?" Often moments I overlooked took on deeper meaning. Then I began to pray in the morning. I am more attentive to the Spirit in the morning, and I seem to prioritize the activity of the day better. That's how the Holy Spirit leads me today.

Some years ago, I wrote a book advising those preparing for confirmation to try reflective prayer as part of their fifty-day preparation for confirmation. I have done this myself for the last eight years as part of my personal preparation to celebrate Pentecost. I record my thoughts each day in a journal, and I try to restrict myself to less than three sentences each day. It has been a great source of blessing for me and for others who are searching for a way to respond better to the Holy Spirit.

The book was recently revised. I rearranged the selection of biblical texts, and also included the text of my journal, summarizing the first seven entries. The empty lined page opposite each text invites others to do the same.

Repeating the same exercise for successive years surprised me. I did not expect to find new, richer meaning each successive year, but that is what happened. Each year finds me in a new context, and I suspect that growing in the Holy Spirit continues to bring new depths to my reflections.

One day I asked young children what they thought the Holy Spirit does. A first-grader responded, "He beeps." That is the most profound word I know of to describe how the Holy Spirit relates to me. He gets my attention — He beeps. Sometimes He goes on to stir me to overcome condemnation. Sometimes He simply moves my heart toward Jesus and His Church. Often it is hard to find the right word to express what the beeps mean, but it is clear that the Holy Spirit is getting my attention. In time of reflective prayer, I tend to see more clearly what that beep is about. The Holy Spirit can use a loud siren that gets the attention of many people at once. But far more common for me is the quiet beep in the depth of my being. That's the sacred space where God dwells.

Jesus recommends that we be like Mary. "Blessed rather are those who hear the word of God and keep it" (Luke 11:28). The sacred space at the center of our being is where each of us is most unique. We have control of the door that admits persons there. That is where our bonds with others develop. When we invite the Holy Spirit there regularly and commune with Him, He makes Jesus more present.

That was Mary's experience, and it can be ours.

Bishop Joseph McKinney is auxiliary bishop of Grand Rapids, Michigan.

15

Loss

by Sally Lynch

"That heart of His, that heart that is called 'sacred' and 'merciful': who can resist it?"

Prayer is a relationship that, for me, was forever changed one day twenty-two years ago. On that day, I had taken my young husband to the hospital to have surgery for advanced malignant melanoma, a seriously life-threatening form of cancer.

The day had been full of busy-ness — arranging for the care of our four young children, talking to teachers at school, packing a hospital suitcase, going through hospital admission procedures, making the frantic trip back home to check on the children and calm their fears, and returning to the hospital. When I finally left the hospital late that evening, the reason for the hectic day's events began to sink in and my heart filled with fear.

I could not lose my husband. I had been too close to death too often in the last three years. My father, my brother — losses I had barely begun to deal with. I could not lose my husband.

I remember getting into the car in the hospital parking lot with heaviness in my heart and a prayer on my lips. "Dear God, I give You my life completely, if only You will spare Marty's."

In that moment, I became aware of a tangible presence, and I saw that it was Jesus before me. In the communion of His heart with mine, I received His assent to the bargain I had just offered in the form of a simple prayer: my life for Marty's. And in that communion of hearts, I knew that not only would Marty's life be spared but that my life would never be the same, that it was no longer mine. This encounter with mercy introduced me to an experience of love I had never known before. Such a big response to such a little prayer. Or was it such a little prayer?

I had prayed throughout my life for special needs. I believed that God heard me when I prayed. When I had become a Catholic at the age of twenty-two, was baptized, and experienced a deeper awakening to God, I prayed more frequently. But this night was different because I came away with a new relationship — not simply new ideas or feelings.

From that night onward, new words gave expression to that new relationship. "I love You, Jesus." I woke up in the morning with these words whispering the foundation of each new day's events. I drifted to sleep at night hearing the echo of these words in the shadows of each day's-end review. "I love You, Jesus."

I began to attend prayer meetings with Marty after his cancer healing. I remember the enthusiasm of the people around me, singing and praying in tongues, and I remember wondering, sometimes, why there was so much noise. Jesus was right there, and all I wanted was for Him to know that we loved Him. "We love You, Jesus." "I love You, Jesus."

Lent arrived within a few months of my initial encounter

with Jesus. That Lent continues to have a profound effect on my prayer life. Throughout the entire forty days, I was given the eyes to see the passion and death of Jesus. For several days, I found myself in the garden of Gethsemane with Him. I could hear Him breathe, see the anguish on His face and the sweat on His brow, watch His trusted companions falling asleep one by one. I knew the betrayal of Judas, the denial of Peter. I followed Him on the walk to Calvary. I saw the torn flesh, the rivers of blood. I heard the taunting. I watched as the nails were driven into His hands and feet, and I witnessed the excruciating death of my Lord.

I grieved a new grief that Lent. It was a grief saturated in love. It was as if I had two programs going on in me at the same time, two tracks playing at once. There was the somber grieving track and there was the awesome loving track. What love the Father has, that He allows His son to suffer and die for me; what love Jesus has, that He conforms His will to His Father's; what love the Holy Spirit has, that He opens these mysteries of suffering and love to my unworthy view.

Having been permitted to touch this Lenten reality in the flesh, so to speak, I was touched by a grace that formed the words to one of the last prayers I have been able to utter for myself:

"Don't ever allow me to forget my first days with You, my Lord, especially these forty days. Don't ever allow me to forget what You have done for me, and what I have promised You. For the rest of my days, no matter what they bring, I want to be faithful to your will for me, so allow me to enter into your heart and your mind. Let me share in your suffering, for the sake of love."

The trajectory of my spiritual life was set during those crucial days, culminating with Eastertide more than two decades ago. To tell the truth, these years have not been easy for me and my husband.

As established mental health clinicians, Marty and I saw from the beginning the urgency of integrating the life-giving truths of our Catholic faith with the graces of the charismatic renewal and the practice of professional mental health care. In our efforts to bring the concept of psycho-spiritual integration to life, we have participated in a most remarkable journey and have seen living proof that "it works."

The journey has not been without its costs. We have suffered severe financial losses; separation from precious children, friends, and community; multiple accidents and health problems; exhausting frustrations and thwartings at every turn.

Our most recent disappointment over the closing of Divine Mercy Treatment Center, a Catholic psychiatric facility we were involved in, has caused many of our friends to question our perseverance for so long in the face of such unremitting opposition.

In fact, it is tempting to give up when something that has borne good fruit is cut down before your eyes or is caused to wither for lack of support. Yet when I come before the Lord in silence, heartbroken and grieving over the consequences of these years on our personal lives, I am quickly reminded of those first days with Him. I remember my prayer to know His heart and to share in His suffering. Mercifully, my lips still utter those well-worn words, "I love You, Jesus," and my grieving heart knows the deep joy of answered prayer.

Even now, as I am putting these thoughts into writing, I find myself all alone in a home we are about to lose. Marty is spending a month in another state looking for work. Our children are married and scattered, looking to follow God's will for them elsewhere. It is a time of endings and uncertain beginnings, and I know a loneliness I have not felt before.

As I confide with Jesus, He reminds me that He, too, is alone and in pain. He shows me a bigger picture, and I insert my little piece into its place. Once again He has allowed me to enter His heart.

So where am I after all these years? I would like to believe that I have grown and developed spiritually, and I suppose in some fairly obvious ways my prayer life has changed, "matured." There is an enhanced flavor of Catholic piety in my prayer and worship preferences; I have met and embraced the mother of Jesus, and I relate to her as my own; my eyes are dazzled by Jesus-in-the-flesh at the Eucharist.

Inevitably, however, I would have to say that I am not too far from my starting point when it comes to the content, if not the form, of my prayer. When I say, "I love You, Jesus," I am saying it with an informed consent seasoned by a broad spectrum of experiences that include empathy with His suffering.

There is no doubt that resting in the heart of the Lord at any given moment may well expose me to some of the pain that His heart knows, pain that is painful and pain that is to be lived. But that heart of His, that heart that is called "sacred" and "merciful": who can resist it?

No matter what, "I love You, Jesus."

Sally Lynch, a psychotherapist in Rochester, New York, has four adult children.

16

As the Bombs Burst

by Dan O'Neill

"As the marble floors shook beneath our feet, I froze in my tracks and began to pray: 'Hail Mary, full of grace . . .' "

When the bombs began to fall, I began to pray. It was June 6, 1982. I was going down the stairway in the Beau Rivage Hotel in West Beirut to take Mercy Corps International's private fact-finding delegation to meet high-ranking members of Lebanese and Palestinian governing authorities in an effort to better understand one of the Middle East's most persistent, bitter, and bloody conflicts. Lebanon had endured a decade of devastating civil war, domination by Syria, and repeated Israeli air strikes.

Mercy Corps International, a Christian relief agency, had become involved in peacemaking ventures in the heart of the war-torn Middle East. Our ministry is based on the corporal works of mercy — the context in which we offered medical aid to hurting people in that tortured land. Our work continues to this day.

As I headed down to the lobby of the stately old hotel, I was flanked by Assemblies of God and Presbyterian ministers who were part of our team. Without warning, sonic booms, bomb bursts, and antiaircraft fire suddenly shattered the late afternoon calm as the Israeli military launched a surprise air attack against PLO forces based in the region. A full-scale armored invasion soon followed, with its infamous siege of Beirut. We were literally across the street from the biggest target of all: PLO headquarters. A precarious situation indeed.

As the marble floors shook beneath our feet, I froze in my tracks and began to pray: "Hail Mary, full of grace . . ."

This prayer caught my two pastor friends by surprise. To be honest, I even startled myself! At a moment when they had looked to me for leadership in providing an earnest, spontaneous prayer for protection in the midst of an obviously serious crisis, I found myself uttering an ancient prayer to the Mother of God. Hardly a gesture of consolation in the face of traditional Protestant sensibilities.

This was a turning point in my prayer life. It was, for me, a previously unexperienced spiritual reflex that became my first automatic Catholic prayer since my conversion to Catholicism a year earlier. My personal Catholic moment had finally arrived. And in a most unexpected fashion.

My minister friends were concerned, to say the least, especially when I reached the end of that timeless Hail Mary prayer: ". . . pray for us sinners, now and at the hour of our death. Amen."

In retrospect, I now realize that my prayer life, almost imperceptibly at first, had begun to change. And I observed an interesting crossroads within the Catholic charismatic experience. While my charismatic Catholic brothers and sisters had become more informal, conversational, and enthusiastic in their prayer lives, I had become more subdued and traditional; that is, gradually engaging the classic, written prayers of the Church as a part of my own personal prayer experience. First at Mass, then in my daily devotional life, I entered into the liturgy and structured historical Catholic prayers with a new level of interior assent. I began to love and cherish the words and phrases that Mother Church had provided in all her ancient wisdom, bequeathed to us by the community of faith.

Not that my spontaneous daily prayer experience had diminished. I simply found myself whispering traditional Church supplications with ever-increasing regularity and comfort. Some of my Protestant friends have wondered if this borders on the dangerous edge of becoming "vain repetition," particularly with such devotional practices as praying the Rosary. I have agreed that, indeed, repetition is a feature of such prayers. But it is not *vain* repetition. Breathing, for example, is highly repetitious, yet life-sustaining. The same holds true in spiritual disciplines that enhance our interior life.

Today, I continue a personal devotional prayer format begun nearly a decade ago. I begin my morning prayer time with the Jesus Prayer as a centering moment, in which I acknowledge my humanity, my frailty, my sins: "Lord Jesus Christ, Son of God, Savior of the world, have mercy on me, a sinner."

Subsequently, I pray the Our Father, relishing each phrase and exploring new possible meanings, as applied to my life: "Our Father, who art in heaven, hallowed be thy name. Thy Kingdom come, thy will be done on earth as it is in heaven. Give us this day our daily bread; and forgive us our trespasses as we forgive those who trespass against us; and lead us not into temptation, but deliver us from evil. For thine is the kingdom and the power and the glory forever and ever. Amen."

Then, after reading the Gospel text for the day, which provides a sense of global participation with the rest of the Church, I contemplate the passage of Scripture for a few moments in silence, and ask God's guidance in applying its relevance to my life.

Following a few personal prayers of special intentions, I close my morning devotional time with that prayer that had come to mean so much in the fires of war we experienced in Lebanon — the Hail Mary: "Hail, Mary, full of grace, the Lord is with thee; blessed art thou among women, and blessed is the fruit of thy womb, Jesus. Holy Mary, Mother of God, pray for us sinners, now and at the hour of our death. Amen."

Of course, like precious stones framing the beginning and ending of my daily prayer experience is the defining Catholic prayer: "In the name of the Father, and of the Son, and of the Holy Spirit," in which we acknowledge the Trinity, trace the cross of Christ, and recall the incomparable moment of our own sacrament of baptism.

As I attempt to live out my faith in a world gone badly awry, this fast-moving culture filled with a cacophony of competing voices that vie for our attention, the timeless treasure of ageless Catholic prayers has become an anchor of stability and the occasion for comfort in my life.

It is how I pray now, at this point in my pilgrimage of faith. I'm certain my prayer life will continue to evolve over time as the Holy Spirit leads me through life's passages, and as I explore the unfathomable wealth of wisdom our Church offers to those who ask, seek, and knock.

Dan O'Neill, father of five young children, is president of Mercy Corps International, a Christian humanitarian-relief organization.

17

Growing Up

by Regina Doman

"God directed the charismatic impulse in me."

You could call me a prime example of a "second-generation charismatic." My parents were baptized in the Holy Spirit at the beginning of the Catholic charismatic renewal and raised me and my numerous siblings in the charismatic manner. I was praying in tongues before I was in Catholic grammar school, and Friday night prayer meetings were a regular part of our family schedule for a good part of my childhood. Later, we joined a charismatic covenant community, and I went on to share in the lives of two more such communities. I attended high school youth conferences at the Franciscan University of Steubenville, and later, the university itself for college. Basically, the charismatic way of prayer — exuberant praise, subdued vocal worship, raised hands, dancing, spontaneous Scripture readings — is second nature to me.

In addition, I am by nature an impulsive, artistic, "creative-type" person. Charismatic worship, with its free-flowing forms, suits my temperament like a glove. As a young person, I enjoyed the chance to channel my enthusiasm into intense prayer when I felt in the mood, or to adopt a more tranquil attitude when I was feeling mellow. The charismatic movement allowed me to channel my emotions and my creativity into prayer. Hence, my artistic side was connected to my "spiritual side" by many strong bonds.

When I was a teenager, I was told by my youth group leaders that I should strive for a daily prayer time. As a single person, I tried to have a least twenty minutes or an hour set aside for prayer every day. But I found it excruciatingly difficult to make myself pray at the same time each day. I hated structure and resented discipline. Even today, I fight my knee-jerk reaction to resist discipline of any kind. Eventually, I settled on a compromise. I knew as a Christian that I needed discipline, artistic temperament or not, and I was going to pray and do it daily.

But, I said to myself, that didn't mean I had to have a prayer time just like everyone else's.

One wise spiritual director told me years later, "Pray as you can, not as you can't." That was what I decided to do. I rejected formal prayers or reading one daily devotional book in favor of a more free-form approach. I began every prayer time by reading a passage of Scripture. In the beginning, I went through the Gospels chapter by chapter, but later I simply opened up to any passage of Scripture I felt moved to look at, just as I was in the habit of flipping through the Bible during prayer meetings seeking a "word from the Lord."

After I had read the Scripture for a little bit, I would open my journal and begin my favorite part of praying. In my notebook, I would jot down a few thoughts on the Scripture, if I felt so moved. Or sometimes I would use the Scripture as a foundation to launch into a poem, story, or play. Other days, I would write a letter to the Lord, pouring out my feelings, my frustrations, my hurts. In my teenage days, I spent many happy hours journaling away in prayer under the gaze of the Lord. I had come to know God as my loving Father, and I was confident that whatever I was interested in, He would also be interested in, even if it was not particularly "spiritual."

For years, the free-form pattern of journaling was my model for prayer. Despite my contentment with it, I still suspected I was being highly unorthodox for writing scripts during my prayer time, and several times guiltily confessed to spiritual mentors that this was the "only way" I could make myself pray daily. Most of them encouraged me, although some did say they were glad that I read the Scriptures first.

However, I could see that some elements were lacking. I envied the discipline my friends and mentors seemed to have in their personal prayer. But Catholic devotions such as the Rosary or reading the lives of the saints turned me off. I resented the duty of going to Mass, and even my practice of reading the Scriptures.

One day, a friend enthusiastically told me how he was memorizing whole passages of the Bible in prayer, and I felt a real twinge of frustration with my own loose approach. "Lord, I want to be able to memorize Scriptures," I muttered to myself later. "Can you help me — somehow?"

And He did, but not without much work on my part. A few days later, I gritted my teeth and got out some index cards, wrote down Scriptures I thought I should know, and tried to go for it. My first attempt was a miserable failure, and I threw out the cards and took out the Bible again. This time, I went through and picked whatever verses from the Gospels struck me and tried to memorize them. I had better success, and was cheered by it. Gradually, I memorized a favorite psalm, and certain passages from the book of Isaiah. I found, to my delight, that the Lord was growing in me a love of the Scripture that hadn't been there before. Perhaps He worked on my love of poetry — once I realized that the psalms and other wisdom books were poetry, I read them with a deeper hunger.

But I still struggled with other kinds of prayer — such as the Rosary. Part of it came from a misunderstanding of Marian theology. Still, even after I learned the reasons behind calling Mary "our life, our sweetness, and our hope," I wasn't any more enthusiastic about this long, drawn-out prayer I had been subjected to since grade school (those Rosaries prayed standing in the classroom before school began seemed to go on for hours). Sadly, I had none of the natural tenderness toward our Blessed Mother that I saw in other Catholics. However, praying the Rosary was something good to do. All sorts of Catholics recommended it — including folks such as the pope and Mother Teresa. At last, I was convinced that even if I disliked the prayer, I should at least try it. I steeled myself and tried to pray the Rosary once a week during Lent.

Praying the Rosary proved even harder for me than reading Scripture. I seethed and struggled and moaned through it. Instead of a moving meditation on the life of Christ, it was for me much more like twenty minutes of serial distractions. I began to suspect that it really was a prayer of vain repetition after all. I certainly couldn't get anything out of it. Every once in a while, I would tell Our Lady guiltily, "Mary, I love you. Please forgive me for hating the Rosary!" Then two things happened. First, I discovered the scriptural Rosary. For me, Scripture provided the link between the life of Christ I knew I should be thinking of and the Mother of God I felt I couldn't relate to. Second, I began praying the Rosary in the car on my way to and from work. Later I kept the book of Scripture verses beside me in the car to glance at, so that I could memorize them. Once I made a habit of praying the Rosary in the car, I was amazed at how my antagonism toward the prayer eased. The mule inside me quieted, and I even joined the Legion of Mary as an associate member, which meant I was committed to praying the Rosary daily. No longer a chore, it was a discipline I appreciated.

I have similar stories about other set devotions, such as the Mass, Bible study, novenas, and the Liturgy of the Hours. One by one, God opened my heart to each of these traditional ways of prayer, and I discovered them afresh.

Now I am a young wife and mother. My life is much busier than my life as a single woman, and it's hard to find time for personal prayer. And I know that babies and small children will make it difficult to get in an hour of prayer all at once.

But God's gift to me in this hour is a husband who has a strong devotion to his prayer life. Although "Spirit-filled," he comes from a family that values the traditional devotions over the more charismatic ones. He insists we pray the Rosary every day, is faithful to his night prayers, including the Divine Office, and makes daily Mass together a priority. Now, if it weren't for the Mass and our family Rosary, some whole days — weeks! — would slip by without my getting a prayer time longer than a few seconds.

Looking back, I can see how God directed the charismatic impulse in me to provide me with a foundation that grew as I grew. He transformed my resentment of Scripture into a delight that still remains with me. I love praying the Scriptures in conjunction with the Rosary, and now that I am a mother, I am finding myself looking more and more to the Mother of Christ. I admit I am still learning to appreciate the Mass, although my reverence for the Eucharist has grown by leaps and bounds.

Still, there is a place for my old ways of prayer. During our "family adoration" of the Blessed Sacrament on Sundays, I am able to come into the presence of my King in the Eucharist, read the Office of the Day, then take out my journal, and write. I still write poems, meditations, diary entries, and even plays before the Eucharist. It has been fruitful to see how He used my free-form prayer times to establish my artistic life as an outgrowth of prayer. And how He led me to the "traditional devotions" to anchor my prayer during the times when my life would be more hectic.

All in all, I am grateful that Our Lord, in His generosity,

like the beneficent steward in the Gospel, has "brought out things from his storehouse both old and new" to enrich my life. I feel, between the two, I have begun to realize the fullness of our faith.

Regina Doman is a freelance author and cartoonist and young mother in Front Royal, Virginia. She is a columnist for the Catholic youth magazine You!

18

Finding Genuine Meditation

by Father Giles Dimock, O.P.

"As the old peasant said when the Curé d'Ars asked him what he was doing in church all day, 'I look at Him and He looks at me.'"

Ultimately, it is the Spirit that prays in us, as St. Paul assures us (Romans 8:26-27), so prayer is God's action in us, but we can cooperate by disposing ourselves to pray.

That is what we do when we say the Lord's Prayer, found in the second chapter of the Gospel of Luke, or the Hail Mary. We say the prayer with our lips, consider the meaning of the words with our mind, and allow that to echo in our heart. These very same prayers can be holy mantras providing a rhythm of prayer against which background the mind meditates on the Mysteries of the Rosary. Here the scenes are the events of the life of Christ and His Mother, by which we are saved. And as the scenes are imagined, the mind draws truths from the Mysteries, which we apply to our lives and savor in our hearts. The Rosary is an excellent combination of vocal prayer and meditation, leading to contemplation, or rest in God.

Today, however, because the Catholic tradition of mysticism is not being taught, many who desire meditation and a life of prayer are drawn to Zen, transcendental meditation, and various forms of oriental techniques they either try to accommodate to Christian piety or simply take up as they leave their Catholic Faith behind. They do not know that there is a rich heritage of mystical experience in the Church, and that the saints, who are our masters in prayer, can teach us how to meditate.

I would like to share the ancient monastic method of meditation, based on their insights, which I use to dispose me for the gift of prayer.

First, one ought to find a quiet place where one can pray undisturbed — a quiet corner of one's room or garden. A church or chapel before the Blessed Sacrament is marvelous, but often one cannot find one open these days. The place I pray is my room, because I am easily distracted by people coming and going in the chapel. My tools are the Bible (it's usually best to start with the New Testament), and often another simple book of devotion or spirituality. The Scepter Press series, "Conversations with God," is most helpful for me now, but I use many different books, according to the season of my life or that of the liturgical year.

I begin by trying to "put myself in the presence of God" by reminding myself that God is within my soul by grace, God who is loving Father, the Redeemer and the Holy Spirit, all loving me and wanting to communicate with me even more than I do with God.

This awareness leads to adoration or praise, in which I'm led to think of the greatness of God the Creator, Redeemer, and Sanctifier, and thank Him and praise Him for all He's done for me in general — bringing me into existence, preserving me, protecting me, etc. — but also in particular — for giving me this family, these friends, saving me from this sin, etc. Praise and adoration sets up the proper stance before God, who loves us and yet is the absolute Lord of heaven and earth, while we are but creatures. We are not only creatures, but sinners who have committed many sins that try to crowd God out of our lives, or flout His law, so we need to repent or express our contrition. I often think of past sins, recent sins, or even reflect on what I might easily be or do without His grace.

The aim is not necessarily to feel the emotion of sorrow, but to resolve to change, to allow myself to be converted. Humility flows from such reflections.

Now I'm ready to consider the truth of the teaching of Jesus in His word by reading, or what the monks called *lectio*. I select a passage in the Gospels — perhaps that of the day — and read it slowly, allowing the words to sink in. A phrase might pop out of the text and I might linger over or ponder that "word" in my heart early in the morning and come back to it during the day.

This is *meditatio*. Some text of Scripture might portray a scene from the Lord's life — a miracle, for example. Some might want to picture the scene and place themselves in the action and allow the Spirit to lead their thoughts. This tends not to work for me. Whether we simply turn a phrase over in our hearts or use our imagination, we should be open to the work of the Spirit praying within, stirring our affections, drawing our will closer to God. Sometimes nothing much will happen, and that's fine, because prayer is not automatic, and we must remember that we dispose ourselves as best we can, but we don't control God any more than we do our friends in a good relationship.

My novice master, in such a situation, would simply say, "Brother, read on" — the Scriptures or some other pious book that has the spirit of God's word — "At least you're doing your spiritual reading," and I in my stumbling attempts to pray find that very consoling.

Often when we have been faithful to prayer, we will experience a deeper prayer that will stir up our faith, hope, and love or move us to ask for some grace. That is what the ancients called *oratio*. Sometimes we will simply rest in the Lord in a way that goes beyond words or concepts. Such is *contemplatio*, a gift more given than many realize, when we're drawn to God by love. As the old peasant said when the Curé d'Ars asked Him what he was doing in church all day, "I look at Him and He looks at me."

When the prayer is drawing to a close after twenty minutes or a half hour, I begin to conclude, thanking God for His presence (for He was present, whether experienced or not), for any graces or insights into my life, or the truths of the faith.

At the end of prayer I intercede for others: family and friends and their needs; the world and its peace; my order; the Church and the pope; and finally my own needs. I present my prayer list to my loving Father, who always gives me what I need, though not always what I want.

I've come to the end of my prayer for now and the end of the method of the ancient monks. Having a way of prayer (and one should use whatever works) is helpful, even when I only experience dryness, because I know I've done what I could; I've disposed myself as well as I could, and in this dry time God wanted me simply to wait in loving and humble faith. Fidelity to prayer each day yields a rich harvest in my life.

I pray early in the morning before our community liturgical morning prayer, because if I don't do it then, it normally won't get done. Late at night might provide some time, but I find that I'm so exhausted by the frantic pace of university life that I'm too tired for meditative prayer. I can attend the Vespers and Compline, say a Rosary, but the structures given help carry the tired mind and body along then.

Often busy parents must sandwich in little prayer breaks

during the day. Their jobs or kids won't permit uninterrupted periods of prayer. Mom must pray while nursing the baby, or dad on the way to work, and praying the Rosary with decades here and there throughout the day can be a wonderful mini-contemplative prayer. I often say decades while crossing the campus or driving — touches of contemplation throughout the day. I've come to love this form of prayer, which I snobbishly avoided for years. It often gives me insights for preaching when prayed in homily preparation.

When all is said and done, one learns to pray by praying as I, in my poor way, struggle to do. And the voice of my eccentric old novice master still rings in my ears as he spoke about prayer — "Brothers, you have to begin."

Father Giles Dimock, O.P., is professor of liturgy at Franciscan University of Steubenville.

19

Out Loud

by Father Thomas Weinandy, O.F.M. Cap.

"I am still a beginner at prayer. I believe that God wants to make prayer exciting for beginners."

Igrew up in a very Catholic environment — a small town in northwest Ohio that was eighty percent German and eighty percent Catholic. Prayer was an intimate part of my childhood. Besides morning and evening prayers, I went to Mass every day, since it was part of the schedule of the Catholic school I attended. I continued this practice even during the summer. Frequently on Sunday afternoons, my family would drive around the countryside visiting and praying at the neighboring churches and shrines. These Sunday pilgrimages would inevitably end up in the neighboring Catholic town at a small bar (we were, after all, *German* Catholics) called the Dew Drop Inn. My dad would have a Limburger cheese sandwich and a beer, my brother and I would have butterscotch sundaes and Cokes, and my mom would have — of all things — a beer and a butterscotch sundae.

The Lord first spoke to me in prayer on my First Communion day when, on the advice of the sister teaching second grade, I asked the Lord what He wanted me to be when I grew up. He said: "I want you to be a missionary priest." I was quite disappointed, because at the time I wanted to be a cowboy. Nonetheless, I remained faithful to the Lord's word, and at the age of fourteen entered a Capuchin seminary. In the seminary, daily Mass and formal prayer were part and parcel of the daily routine.

My early seminary years were happy ones, but during my novitiate year and my subsequent years of college and theology, I became more and more aware that my life with Jesus — and thus my life of prayer — were not what they should be. I did not doubt my faith. Rather, it was precisely *because* of my faith that I felt something was not quite right. If Jesus was the risen Lord and Savior and if I was a temple of the Holy Spirit and God was my Father, why then did I not experience these truths? At first, I thought it was because I lacked holiness — which I did. But then, after reading lives of the saints, I realized that these men and women first experienced Jesus and only then became holy. I realized that, if I was to become holy and to pray as they prayed, then I too must first experience Jesus.

Being a rather reserved and shy person, I considered the charismatic renewal as something for extroverts. However, I saw that those in the renewal did know Jesus, and so with some fear and trembling I asked, in May of 1975, a Capuchin confrere to pray over me for the baptism in the Spirit. By this time I had been ordained a priest for three years and was living in London, finishing my doctorate in historical theology.

The baptism in the Spirit changed my life. Jesus came alive. I experienced the love of the Father. I knew the life and power of the Holy Spirit. The whole gospel took on a reality I never knew before. Through the baptism in the Spirit, I experienced the bright day of my soul. I rejoiced in the new life of the Spirit. On more than one occasion, the Lord has told me that I must always be faithful to the grace of the baptism in the Spirit.

The consequences of the baptism in the Spirit on my prayer life were — and continue to be — immense. I would like to specify some of the changes here.

First, I always knew I should praise and glorify Jesus. Only after the baptism, when Jesus came alive for me in His glory, was I truly able to do so. I want to emphasize, then, the importance of vocal praise. It was the vocal nature of praise that nurtured my relationship with Jesus and continues to do so. To praise and to glorify Jesus out loud (genuinely out loud and not in muted, embarrassed whispers), with fullness of voice and thus with the fullness of being, nurtured within me the love for Jesus and the acknowledgment of who He is as my only Lord and Savior. The more I wholeheartedly praised Jesus, the more real He became to me. The more I praised Him in personal prayer and at prayer meetings, the more I was committed to Him.

I have learned then that vocal praise is not to be belittled as second-rate prayer. The same story recurs in the lives of saints. Someone goes into a church where they pray all night. The next morning they say, "I saw Francis (or some other saint) wrapped in prayer and I *heard* him pray all night!" I doubt whether any saint has grown in prayer without vocal praise. I believe that it is through vocal praise of Jesus that we can come to the heights of union with God.

A second way that my prayer has changed likewise flows from the impact of vocal praise. In the midst of praise, the Spirit reveals to me more deeply the truths of the gospel. The reason is quite simple. In praise, we turn away from ourselves to the mysteries of our faith. By focusing our attention through praise on the mysteries and doctrines of our faith, the Spirit can lead us to a greater depth of understanding and experience.

For example, if I intensely praise Jesus for becoming man, then the reality of the incarnation takes on a new intensity in my life. Or if I praise Jesus for dying on the cross that I might be freed from sin and cleansed in His blood, or if I glory in His resurrection, then the whole work of redemption — the power of the cross, the cleansing in Jesus' blood, the new life of His resurrection — becomes more alive for me. Likewise, it is in the midst of praising God the Father for being my Father that I come to see more clearly why God is my Father and what it means for me to be His son.

I receive revelation in the midst of praise and worship of God in His mysteries. This revelation has become so important in my own daily life. Through revelation in prayer, the realities of God can become more real for us than the things of this world. Because of this revelation, I can more easily live with an awareness of the realities of heaven, knowing that Jesus is my Lord and Savior, and that through the indwelling of the Holy Spirit I am a son of the Father. As St. Paul states: "Set your minds on things that are above, not on this that are on earth" (Colossians 3:2).

Third, I have found that one of the most important aspects of prayer is timing. I have grown in prayer, in Scripture reading, in love for and knowledge of the mysteries of the faith, because I have learned to be faithful to a daily prayer time. If I get up in the morning and do not know when I am going to pray during that day, I am sure that I will not pray that day. Only because I have scheduled a daily prayer time — the first hour after I get up — am I assured that I will pray. It is no longer a matter of whether I feel like praying or not. God has blessed and honored this commitment. I know that if I come to God in daily prayer, the Spirit will touch my heart and my mind.

I am still a beginner at prayer. I believe that God wants to make prayer exciting for beginners. He wants us to be expectant about what He will do for us in prayer. God wants to reveal His love and mercy to beginners. He wants us to leave prayer joyful and full of life and eager to assume the tasks He sets before us each day.

When we mature in prayer, some of us may experience the dark night of the soul. But for me and for almost all of us, I am convinced that for now God wants us to experience in prayer the bright day of our soul where we experience the abundant love of the Father, the glory and majesty of Jesus, His Son, and the life and vibrancy of the all-powerful Holy Spirit.

Father Thomas Weinandy, O.F.M. Cap., is Warden of Greyfriars Hall in Oxford, England, and lectures in history and doctrine at Oxford University.

20

In the Stillness

by Henry Libersat

"At age sixty the big difference is an awareness of just how close God is to me."

Prayer is the language of a love affair with God. Today, at age sixty, I talk to God differently than I used to.

I first began to pray at my mother's knee. I memorized and recited back to her the required prayers for First Communion: Our Father; Hail Mary; Glory Be; Acts of Faith, Hope, Love, and Contrition; the Creed. Of course, I had little idea of what those prayers meant, but I prayed them as prayers.

I think God rejoiced in them, perhaps more than in some of my "prayers" today. I now know more about what words mean and how good God is, but I'm so often distracted. When the child looks into his daddy's eyes and says, "Da-Da," he doesn't know all that the name enfolds. He doesn't know he came from his father's and mother's love, that his parents work for him, even slave for him, put up with misery for him. But the father hears "Da-Da" and rejoices. That's more and more my image of God as He hears my poor murmurs.

I've prayed for most of my life. There was a period following the Second Vatican Council when I did very little "formal prayer," believing that my entire life was a prayer. My entire life is supposed to be a prayer, but sometimes it is a gripe and grumble, and even a rebellious excursion away from God.

But I pray very differently today than I used to. I still pray formal prayers: the Rosary, the Liturgy of the Hours, including morning and evening prayer. The big difference is an awareness of just how close God is to me. To be sure, I don't feel worthy of His presence, but I do feel a deep gratitude.

My "prayer stance" is one of grateful repentance. Grateful because God has made me, redeemed me, introduced me to Jesus as my Savior, and called me into the Catholic Church — all out of love. That gratitude leads into repentance because I want to please God, to cease offending Him by what I do and by what I fail to do.

That's my general attitude in prayer, which is manifested in various ways, such as the following:

In my marriage. Sometimes, when I am sitting alone with my wife and just holding hands, I am suddenly filled with a sense of being so very close to the kingdom and being with God in a special way. That is the grace of the sacrament of matrimony as much as it is the grace of baptism and confirmation. God walks with us and speaks with us in our marriages — sometimes most powerfully when we are silent with one another in His presence.

In nature. At a retreat years ago, a nun once sent us out for some quiet time and told us in so many words, "Go hug a tree." I had been under a lot of pressure. I walked through the woods, began to reflect on St. Francis, and started really looking and touching the trees and flowers. I loved that moment when my focus was directed outward toward other creatures of God rather than inward on poor little me. To this day, I "hug trees."

In the liturgy. The highest point of my prayer life is the official liturgy of the Church. No, it's not always the warmest experience. It's not always an emotional high. In fact, sometimes, it's a real drain. My friend Bert Ghezzi once said that it's easy to go to Mass or to pray when you feel like it. But you know you are really worshiping God, doing what God wants, when you go to Mass even if you don't want to go, even if you're bored, distracted, or angry.

The Mass is my strength. In the Eucharist I come to know God most intimately, and find strength from His grace and my parish community. The Mass brings us all together at the foot of the cross, and we gaze on Jesus as He dies for us, rises for us and gives us Himself in the Eucharist.

Second in prayer power in my life is the Liturgy of the Hours. It's a wonderful consolation to realize I am praying the same prayers so many others in the Church are praying that day — from the Holy Father to the most obscure layperson or cloistered nun in the world.

In confession. The sacrament of reconciliation is a prayer. In confession, I am praying and worshiping. I'm submitting to God. I tell Him that he's right and I'm wrong, he's holy and I'm a sinner. I am praising God because I want to turn away from sin and embrace Him.

The Rosary. I don't pray the Rosary every day, but most days I do. I have acquired a tape of Father Kevin Scallon and Dana reciting all fifteen Mysteries of the Rosary. On my way to work on most days, I pray five Mysteries.

Communion of the saints. I like to pray with the saints — those who have been canonized and those who have not. My litany includes parents, grandparents, uncles, aunts, cousins, in-laws, childhood friends, former pastors and bishops, and fellow parishioners who are now with the Lord. I also include St.

Paul, St. John the Baptist, all four evangelists, my deacon friends — Stephen, Lawrence, Francis, Ephrem, Philip, and Niconar. Also in my litany are my own patrons, Henry, Pierre, and Joseph, as well as those great preachers John Chrysostom and Peter Chrysologus, our parish patron Mary Magdalen, and, of course, our beloved Mother Mary.

In ministry. I pray all the time in my ministry as a deacon: conducting wakes, praying with the sick, with people experiencing various problems. "Ministerial prayer" can be both personal and liturgical. At wakes, for example, our parish has a standard service. We've all heard it many times, but it is always uplifting because it is prayed in faith and in love, in sorrow and in hope.

I've prayed with people who suffered despair and found my own soul renewed as the Lord dispels darkness with His joyous light. One man comes to mind. He came hundreds of miles to pray with me because I had helped Sister Briege McKenna write her bestselling book, *Miracles Do Happen*. The Lord touched us both deeply and he was healed in a special way.

In wordless presence. I don't claim to be a contemplative. Contemplative prayer is a special gift from God, and I don't think you can manufacture it through centering or meditation or any other "form" of prayer. In the end, I believe what Mother Angelica once said to me: "The best way to pray is the way you pray best."

However, I do have those rare and wonderful experiences of God's wordless presence. They come at moments alone on the back patio, or sitting in the woods or in chapel. They come, as I've said, when I'm sitting quietly with my beloved wife, Peg. I've felt that powerful presence as I watched little bean sprouts break through the crust of brown garden earth, or watched a baby chick peck its way out of its shell. I felt this powerful wordless presence when holding a new child or grandchild. Most of all, I've felt this wordless presence sitting before the Blessed Sacrament or receiving Our Lord in Holy Communion.

I used to imitate the way others prayed. It helped me experience different forms of prayer and perhaps helped me develop my present attitude of grateful repentance. More than ever, after all these years of praying and trying to pray better, I am convinced that each of us has to be true to self.

The foundation of prayer is not style or form; it is a willingness to let God in, to let God do, to let God say. It is also a willingness to let God be silent and sometimes seemingly distant.

In those moments when God seems so far away, we have an excellent opportunity to pray on God's terms: to do what God wants when it seems God may not care. That, to me, is what exercising faith is all about. If we have no dry periods, we never exercise our faith, never test our intellectual conviction about God, remain only God's fair-weather friends.

This has been and remains a hard lesson for me. I do not always live up to it, but I think I'm beginning to make progress, even if it's only because I'm older and just too darned tired to rebel as often as I did in the past.

Henry Libersat is editor of The Florida Catholic newspaper, which serves six dioceses in Florida. He is a deacon of the diocese of Orlando.

21

The Most Important Thing

by Father Michael Scanlan, T.O.R.

"Whatever is worthwhile and lasting in my life's activity was first conceived in some way in prayer."

The best way I can express how I pray today is to quote the Holy Father from *Crossing the Threshold of Hope:* "The pope prays as the Holy Spirit permits him to pray."

I find that the Holy Spirit opens and closes doors to prayer. It is the Holy Spirit who anoints in power certain directions in prayer, and it is the Holy Spirit who blocks other avenues. Though I must start prayer, once started it is not my own. As my prayer changes, so does my life. The Holy Spirit reshapes my life through prayer. I don't always cooperate, but when I do, I also see the results in a life change.

I am reminded of the refrain: "Melt me, mold me, fill me, use me." This is in line with the statement in the *Catechism of the Catholic Church*, "We pray the way we live, and we live the way we pray." If we want to change the way we live, we change the way we pray. This is what the Holy Spirit does in us if we yield to Him.

A new sense of prayer comes from the experience of being baptized in the Holy Spirit, which initially leads to a new involvement in praise, an increased desire to pray, and a willingness to pray in the Spirit rather than predominantly in mental prayer.

In my life this new development meant an increase of prayers of praise followed by quiet prayer of rest in God's presence. It also meant dwelling more on the words of Scripture and yielding to the power of those words to touch my spirit and change me. It included a new awareness of praise based on the power of the Holy Spirit. In a special way, it also included the use of the charismatic gifts of tongues, inspiration, and revelation as a normal part of daily prayer. In time, I saw an overall approach develop that became a pattern I could teach. I outlined this pattern (which was based on analogy to a business meeting) and published it in the booklet *Appointment with God* (Franciscan University Press).

My prayer has continued to change within this broad outline, as the Holy Spirit anointed some directions and closed off others. Frequently, the areas where I needed to repent, change direction, or give new commitments were the only ones with a sense of anointing or power. After I would respond, change would happen and then new areas would become anointed. Sometimes this process took many months before there was movement to a new area.

I experienced this process moving me to fervent consecration of life. For a few months, all the power in my prayer and the overwhelming time and effort in my prayer was concentrated on heartfelt consecration of my life. I used the Morning Offering, the DeMontfort Consecration to Jesus through Mary, the Consecration to the Sacred Heart of Jesus, the daily renewal of my vows of poverty, chastity, and obedience, and other prayers of consecration and entrustment.

In a similar way, I experienced months of concentration on intercession where I prayed extensively in tongues after each petition. Some days I could pray for one hour using the petitions that were listed in the morning prayer of the Divine Office. There were other times when a simple quiet presence or regard toward the Lord would occupy me for an hour at a time. I also recall times when every line of Scripture seemed to come alive and grab my inner being.

It wasn't all action, however. There was a period of more than a year when dryness and desolation totally dominated. I experienced being broken and humbled before God much as a person would feel if left hanging from a tree buffeted by wind and rain and all the elements. Prayer changed from an exciting encounter with the living risen Lord to a reaching in the dark to a far distant and seemingly absent Lord.

While the classic manuals on the spiritual life deal with these various phenomena of prayer, the words of the Holy Father gave me the best insights. In *Crossing the Threshold of Hope*, John Paul II gives the context of his own prayer in terms of Romans 8. Verses 18 to 31 are particularly relevant.

Verse 18 expresses the hope that should be in us despite present sufferings: "I consider that the sufferings of this present time are not worth comparing with the glory that is to be revealed to us." The pope particularly refers to the references on groaning. Verses 22 to 23 read, "We know that all creation is groaning in labor pains even until now, and not only that but we ourselves who have the first fruits of the Spirit, we also groan within ourselves as we wait for adoption, the redemption of our bodies. For in hope we are saved."

Writing about his personal prayer, the pope directs the reader to verses 26 and 27: "In the same way the Spirit too comes to the aid of our weakness, for we do not know how to pray as we ought but the Spirit itself intercedes with inexpressible groaning. And the one who searches the heart knows what is the intention of the Spirit because He intercedes for the holy ones according to God's will."

One morning I was privileged to stand next to the Holy Father during his morning Mass, and at the intervals for personal prayer, I could hear him groaning in the Spirit. I've found that the gift of tongues enables me to participate in this "inexpressible groaning" as I intercede.

It is this mixture of sorrow around us and hope within us that leads to the groaning in the Spirit for the full redemption of our lives and our communities, indeed the whole world. The hope that keeps groaning and won't give up is the hope poured out in our heart through the Holy Spirit and the hope expressed in the last verses of Romans 8: "For I am convinced that neither death, nor life, nor angels, nor principalities, nor present things, nor things to come, nor height, nor depth, nor any other creature will be able to separate us from the love of God in Christ Jesus our Lord" (verses 38-39).

I am certain that prayer is the most important thing I do. I believe that whatever is worthwhile and lasting in my life's activity was first conceived in some way in prayer and then given existence in action. It is the necessary foundation of all my apostolic activity. I cannot love rightly, serve faithfully, or make decisions with wisdom unless these flow from prayer. For these reasons, I always use a journal, writing something from each prayer time. I always read the previous day's entry during the next day's prayer. I also make it a daily practice to pray over my schedule for that day. This enables me to come closer to God's perspective and His priorities regarding all that I will be facing that day.

There is so much more I could write. I pray daily the Prayer before the Crucifix, the Rosary, and the Divine Chaplet. I open every meeting which I chair with the prayer Come, Holy Spirit.

I believe that the Holy Spirit indeed comes and fills our hearts and enkindles the fire of His love when we invite Him into our lives and gatherings. I treasure the daily Mass, which I am privileged to celebrate, and the daily Divine Office. I find that the readings in this daily liturgy always have some special application for my life. I schedule myself to go to one special charismatic praise gathering each week.

This is how I pray today. It is God's gift operating as the Holy Spirit permits and changing as God ordains in His merciful love.

Father Michael Scanlan, T.O.R., is president of Franciscan University of Steubenville in Ohio. His many books include What Does GOD Want? A Practical Guide to Making Decisions.

22

In the Desert

by John Michael Talbot

*"It is time to embrace the personal conversion
and prayer of the desert monks."*

After over fifteen years, God is taking me back to the basics. As He did with Hosea the prophet, Jesus Our Lord, and Paul the apostle, the Spirit is leading me back to the desert. I am becoming a student again in the early monastic school of the desert fathers and mothers. Through them I am being born again as a disciple of Jesus Christ.

At the beginning of my Catholic conversion, in 1977 and 1978, I read through the desert fathers and mothers. It was "the thing to do." It was part of being with the contemplative "in crowd." I read the books, I went to the workshops at charismatic conferences. It was a good initial education. I learned the initial lessons of integrating Catholic contemplation and my past evangelical and charismatic roots. It was good in so far as it went.

Then came the real teacher — community. An integrated monastic community of celibate brothers, celibate sisters, and monastic families, called the Brothers and Sisters of Charity, was formed at Little Portion Hermitage. Here the lessons of Scripture and the fathers and mothers of the monastic and Franciscan traditions were really "fleshed out" and learned.

The real lessons came in the kitchen or the laundry room. The "little things" proved the biggest obstacles, such as working in the kitchen with someone who thinks we should do it the way their mother or family taught them . . . or when "they" have done their laundry on your day! These painful encounters of daily life are the proving ground of our greater gospel values. As Jesus said, "If you are faithful in little things, God will give you the great."

When it comes down to the "laundry room" experiences of life, we often fail in actually living the Catholic Christian answer in Christ. Even for the most "renewed" of us, our religion remains a Sunday Mass, weekly prayer or cell group, annual conference, or even daily prayer time. Only for a rare few does it really cut into our typical American, "me first" individualistic lifestyles. Even among "radical" Catholics and Christians, the statistics on divorce, various forms of abuse, or just plain old consumerism remain much the same as, or just barely better than, the secular world.

Over the last fifteen years I have seen hundreds come to community and only a few dozen stay. Many leave through the "revolving door" syndrome, despite promises and vows professed publicly into the hands of a superior, and solemnly witnessed by the Church. Many times I have sat face to face with people who admit that what they are doing is not the perfect will of God, but choose to do it anyway. They say God will forgive them. When the bottom line of "my will" versus the will of God through the community is reached, most will choose their own self-will. In a sense, our individualistic and permissive society has programmed us for exactly this response.

Primitive monasticism and all later communal developments are unanimous that "self will" is one of the devil's favorite tools to destroy communities and individuals who decide to navigate the stormy seas of spiritual warfare alone.

This revolving door has left those of us who faithfully remain in community feeling a bit "bloody and bruised." When commitments are broken, trust and good faith are jeopardized. Those left in the community have used the available Christian counseling tools to process this hurt. Much has healed. We have learned from our mistakes, and had to repent and ask forgiveness on occasion. But there still remains a deep residual hurt in one's spiritual gut . . . like having the wind knocked out of our spiritual sails.

It is at this juncture I picked up the writings of the desert fathers and mothers again. To my utter surprise, I found them speaking to much, if not exactly, the same communal situation as we had experienced. They describe the tragically humorous spiritual and mental process of those who leave. It is uncanny how precisely they describe our modern experience from over one-thousand or even fifteen hundred years ago. Naming the motivation of the eight principal demons of gluttony, lust, avarice, anger, dejection, listlessness, self-esteem, and pride, they get to the real core of the spiritual and emotional issue.

Three demons lead the charge: gluttony, avarice, and self-esteem. Gluttony awakens our fallen senses and leads to lust. Avarice unfulfilled leads to anger, dejection, and the burnout boredom of listlessness. Self-esteem opens the door to the mother of all demons — pride. All lead us away from community, church, and Christ Himself.

Needless to say, this list of demons and vices flies in the face of our modern American, and even Christian, Catholic, and monastic/religious lifestyles. Gluttony — food flows in unheard-of abundance, even in religious circles. Real fasting is rare. Lust — sexual promiscuity, flirtatious behavior, and immodesty are the norm, and even infect communities, seminaries, and religious houses. Avarice — materialism and consumerism are rampant. Anger is the hottest topic on weekday talk shows and for self-help books. Despondency hits many who see modern life as filled with despair. Boredom is immediately experienced if our life is not constantly filled with projects, sights, sounds, tastes, and most importantly, possessions! We are literally consumed in consumerism. Self-esteem is the norm to battle our low self-images rather than allowing ourselves to be conformed to the image of God in Christ. And pride has become the subtle motivation even for our religious acts, especially for those in communities, prayer and devotional groups, and public ministries.

Beyond simple and humble faith in Jesus Christ and the power of the Holy Spirit, the desert fathers and mothers encourage practical and doable disciplines such as spiritual reading, vigils, fasting, and manual labor to help overcome these demons and vices.

In all of this, one experiences deep contrition for one's sins. A new self-awareness is opened up along with a real humility that leads to repentance. This is frequently manifested by the gift of tears. It is helped and facilitated through brief confession of one's tempting and sinful thoughts to your spiritual father or mother (usually the superior of the monastic community). Daily meditation on death (this may be the last day of your life on earth) also encourages a "no nonsense" approach.

The desert masters also describe an extraordinary way to detachment, inner silence, and abiding peace. This is the way of self-accusation. In contrast to, and beyond, modern techniques of self-assertion and the dialogue of conflict resolution, the monks of old simply learned to see all opposition and conflict as our just due for sins. These sins may be known or unknown, related to the conduct of some other. But the way to deeper and abiding inner peace can only be found by accounting all "injustice" towards us as the revelation of God's greater justice for the salvation of our souls. Once we have that inner peace, then proper dialogue and conflict resolution might be undertaken.

Such a way might seem crazy and foolish to the logic of the world, but the monks of old assure us that such an approach is the only way to peace in the intensity of relationships in a monastic community. Instead of beginning with the problems "out there" in others, the desert monks insisted that we must begin ourselves. Of course, they also warn against the devil's favorite tool with overzealous Christians — scrupulosity.

I must say that I have found this rugged and radical "desert way" the most demanding challenge to my modern Catholic Christian and monastic experience I have ever encountered. But it not only challenges, it promises. It also delivers the greatest inner peace in Christ I have ever known when I dare try. Suddenly, yet not without much disciplined practice, a life of real Christian virtue is really stirring in my soul. I admit, it is still rarely seen in my life. I am only a beginner. Please pray for my conversion.

I had seen powerful movements based on charismatic personalities go wrong or simply peter out. The modern mediocre norm of even charismatic and contemplative Christianity had lulled me to sleep. My inner pain from community had led me to this deceptive slumber under the illusion of "God's rest." But now the real contemplative and charismatic saints of the monastic desert of the past have roused me. My spirit and soul have been awakened by their radical life of discipleship in Christ. It has challenged me in places so deep in my soul they cannot be adequately described, and it has challenged my lifestyle. Pray that I continue to respond.

In conclusion you may be asking: Is this really about John Michael's prayer life? It most certainly is, if we see our whole way of life as a prayer. Furthermore, I have discovered that most of us who think of ourselves as charismatic contemplatives really are not. Real charismatic contemplatives barely know it. All they know is God. As St. Benedict says, "Prefer nothing to Christ." They consider themselves the least of all, still struggling with the active life of conversion from their sins. Then, almost unknowingly, they pass over into the stillness and peace of the contemplative life as a true gift from God.

As usual, we Americans want a "fast food" spirituality. But there is no quick and easy answer; it requires time. It requires the discipline of one's whole life. Then we become real charismatic bearers of the Holy Spirit. Many of us consider ourselves "advanced" when we have yet to really make a good beginning. For myself, I am still a mere beginner, struggling to overcome even my most basic sins through Jesus Christ. In this I have found the call to the rugged spirituality of the desert quite challenging and helpful.

Today, so much of our modern society is crumbling. Values are crumbling. The family is crumbling. God help us, even our churches and communities are crumbling. Many are frightened and confused. Many of us have also been burned out in battling this spiritual and moral decay by focusing "out there" in the big bad world. But all too frequently the problem is not "out there"; the problem is within. It is "us" before it is "them."

Perhaps it is time to focus honestly on our own sins and failings and bring them to forgiveness and change in Jesus. Maybe it is time to seek refuge in the hidden desert caves and wadis of the early monastic fathers and mothers. Perhaps it is time to put away all our plans and programs and really embrace the personal conversion and prayer of the desert monks for ourselves. If we really respond to such a radical gospel challenge then we ourselves can be healed in Christ. Then, by the real power of the Spirit, God will restore the Church, our communities and all the world to a glory only known by Him . . . the glory of Jesus Christ, Our Lord.

John Michael Talbot, the songwriter and performer, lives in Eureka Springs, Arkansas.

23

A Patchwork

by Catherine Odell

"Pray as you can, don't pray as you can't."

I think that my first important lesson about prayer came at the age of eight. It was the day of my first Holy Communion, a warm Sunday in early May. Along with about eighty-five other second-graders, I had prepared for this day for many weeks. I had memorized a number of prayers printed on a folded card for the wonderful event. Some were to be said to prepare my soul for the Eucharist; others were thanksgiving prayers, to be said in my pew, right after Jesus had really come to me.

As I was getting dressed, with my First Communion dress and veil lying on the bed, a little flicker of fear began inside of me. I couldn't remember any of the memorized thanksgiving prayers! I had said them over and over again with my class, but now, I realized, they were totally gone, vaporized from my consciousness!

When I found that I hadn't brought my prayer card home from school, I began to weep and moan in panic and despair. How could I receive the Eucharist properly now? My teenage brother Jim finally intervened. When I explained the unfolding tragedy, he said simply, "Oh, Cath, say the prayers in your own words! God understands that too!" Later that morning, I did pray in my own words as Jesus came to me in the Eucharist. I had a sweet feeling of His joy and peace, as well as a deep sense of His real presence.

Jim's advice had made perfect sense to me. I learned that prayer means opening our hearts to God, and also trying to hear God.

But that lesson of my early childhood faded for many years. It seemed more logical, more effective to pray to God with established prayers. Through my childhood, I learned the Rosary, the Mass prayers of course, the Morning Offering, the Angelus, the Memorare, the Creeds, the litanies, and many other wonderful prayers which we said in school.

Not until I became involved in charismatic renewal prayer groups in my early thirties, however, did I feel again that joyful freedom and "permission" I felt on the day of my First Communion. In the renewal, spontaneous prayer, prayer from the heart, the prayer of praise, lifted my prayer from a flat reality. Prayer became three-dimensional. It was real!

At a charismatic prayer meeting, I also received the gift of speaking in tongues. I welcomed it, but perhaps not with great enthusiasm. It has never grown beyond a handful of strange words. I pray in tongues when I'm alone, perhaps while driving or gardening. For me, it's a relaxing way to pray. I simply praise God. I don't have to think about what to say or how to formulate it. God knows what I mean, what I need, and the way I would choose to intercede for others.

I don't attend charismatic prayer meetings now but I will

always be grateful to this movement of spiritual renewal. I began to see that both formal prayer and spontaneous prayer should be part of my prayer life. As an adult, I began to love the Rosary and Mary more.

The advice and experience of others in the charismatic renewal continues to be helpful too. At a prayer meeting one time, I had heard someone say "Pray as you can, don't pray as you can't." That is a very humane, a very realistic bit of advice, because none of us will ever pray perfectly.

Another time, I laughed but also learned a great deal from a story told by Sister Margaret Anne, one of the great nuns in our prayer group. It seems that Jack, a man she knew, was very devoted to intercessory prayer. He had a large family and a demanding job. Periodically, Jack updated a list of all the prayer needs from his family and friends on one large sheet of paper. Each night he would read each intention and pray for that person or need.

One night, however, Jack was terribly exhausted during prayer. He finally took the list and held it high up in the air for God to see. "Here it is, God," he prayed softly, "you know what our needs are. Please answer them." Jack later told Sister Margaret Anne that he felt so freed up and happy when he gave his large list to God. He was just as committed as ever to intercessory prayer, but he realized that taking the time to pray every day was an intercession, even if he didn't name each person or prayer need.

In recent years, I think often about Jack's list thrust into the air. Like Jack, I sincerely desire to intercede for many people. I also once listed them all. All of my family members, my husband's family members, our friends, people who were sick in any way, and the special intentions of my heart were all down in black and white. I also went to daily Mass more than I do now.

I want to return to a more regular prayer time in my life, but that will be challenging now. I am a wife, a mother of two fairly young children, ages three and eight. I work out of my home, and the lines between professional work time and "Mom" time are continually blurred. I am forever juggling jobs. The house is never fully cleaned, the laundry never completely done. I never have enough time to write as much as I should, and the basket of correspondence for the small periodical I edit is seldom empty. I would like to learn Spanish, to get back to painting, and begin to play the guitar. But when?

So, the way I pray now is a true patchwork. I often pray the Rosary — it gives me peace and seems to help me focus. I also pray spontaneously or in tongues throughout the day. I pray for the things I read about in the paper. I scan the articles and pray for a greater respect for children, an end to abortion and wars, wisdom for national and international leaders, and a sense of generosity for our consumer society in the United States. When I go grocery shopping, I pray to buy wisely and that my family will receive true and healthy nourishment from the food we buy and from other "food" in their lives.

I also pray for the people I see who seem troubled or tired. Several months ago, I saw a young mother angrily spanking a little boy who was about two years old. He was howling with huge tears running down his cheeks. Mother and son were in the grocery store late at night. "I bet he's pretty tired," I smiled, trying to look sympathetic for her plight. But I prayed that this would not be a child abuse situation. I prayed that she would somehow be given the skills to understand and deal with her little boy. I prayed because she was there and I was there. God put us there together at that moment for a reason.

Truthfully, prayer emerges in many forms the more we understand one thing. It is God — not chance — who has set each of us into our families and communities to live and love. It's there that we should dwell in peace and joy — and inevitably, then, in prayer.

Catherine Odell, mother of two, is author of Father Solanus, The Story of Solanus Casey *and* Those Who Saw Her: Apparitions of Mary. *She lives in South Bend, Indiana.*

24

With a Broken Heart

by Father Benedict J. Groeschel, C.F.R.

"We are told in the Bible, 'Be still and confess that I am God!' This is absolutely the best method of prayer."

I grew up thinking that prayer was a good work done to express gratitude to God, or repentance, or even to humbly (but very precisely) remind the Divine Being of what I thought was best for the world or for me.

In high school I decided I should move along to something a bit more reflective. For people in my age group, the practice of mental prayer was the very trendy thing just before the Second Vatican Council. We worked at it and it was a big help. I will not review with you all of the steps, but if you're interested, any older Catholic library will produce a copy of *Progress Through Mental Prayer*, by Edward Leen, C.S.Sp.

The idea was to grow spiritually by learning the ability to quietly dissect and apply the truths of faith or Scripture quotations to one's own life. Mental prayer was described as a sermon preached to oneself with room for a personal or affective response. "Affective" meant that one's experience was primarily that of the will, with a discreet touch of emotion.

As I look back on my years of poor performance at "mental prayer," or meditation, I realize that I never did it well. On the so-called three-point meditation, I never once got to the third point. I kept getting lost in distracting thoughts or modest religious experiences that drew me away from one of the three points. I always ended up feeling guilty and inadequate.

In later years I have learned to transform the art of mental prayer into actually preaching sermons. I have never had the courage to listen to one of my sermons on tape, but once when I had to solve a technical problem (blipping out a few sneezes when I had a cold), I realized that I was meditating out loud when I preached. I finally had achieved, in a way, the three-point method.

As the years went on, I got more and more off the track of structured meditation and fell into the slow meditative reading of the great spiritual classics, or even one of the contemporary books written in that style. This kind of meditation was considered something of a second-class enterprise by the mental-prayer enthusiasts of the past, and even by the centering-prayer people at the present time.

It is actually the *lectio divina* of St. Benedict. This meditative reading was used almost universally well into the Middle Ages, and more often than not, was expressed as chant or religious singing. This method is also called Teresian, because the great Madre of the spiritual life used it to control her widely wandering thoughts and powerful imaging faculties. I must say that I am today much more at home with this method, although it is still considered second-class by many.

Some of us learn early and some of us learn late, but most of us learn. I have finally achieved, as a result of reading the great books and prayers of the saints, and near saints, to take the next step, and that is to be quiet and listen. I have discussed this method — if it can be called that — in a little book called *Listening at Prayer* (Paulist Press, 1984). A combination of a life too busy with apostolic commitments and the need to pray often led me to use the most powerful prayer book of all. I had read a powerful line in the *Imitation of Christ* when I was in high school that has haunted me through the years. "If your heart is pure then every creature will be to you a mirror of God and a book of holy teaching."

St. Augustine taught that Christ calls to us by His life, by His death, His resurrection, and by all created things "which stand at the door of our senses and shout 'He made us.' " St. Francis heard God speaking in the sun, the storm, the flowers. Lepers and lambs, doves and wolves, popes and robbers all spoke to him of Christ.

It is not enough simply to try to listen, although that is essential. One must do what a skilled photographer does with a camera: stop life for a moment and stand back and look. But this is just a technique, and techniques alone never lead us to God, just to the illusion that we have found Him. The most important thing with this simple method is to use the words of the *Imitation of Christ*, that is, to have a pure heart.

This expression — "pure heart" — has several important meanings for the person seeking to grow in prayer. The heart refers to the center of our being — the inner place where emotion, memory, mind, and will come together into an utterly unique individual. In the heart, the person rises to God or drags along in mediocrity, or even starts down the road to hell. A heart can be pure, or lackluster, or drab, or dirty, or even rotten. It can be contrite, bruised, broken, crushed, or dead. Your heart may be filled with joy, sorrow, pain, love, hate, fear, or dissipate its energies on all kinds of things and end up like a circus ring. Our hearts, however, are where we must meet God when we love Him or where we can worship false gods, which are really nothing more than pieces of our own egotism painted up with religious symbols. For the Christian a broken and contrite heart is the best, so that the Holy Spirit can create a clean heart within us.

Most of the time we don't even think about the spiritual place we call the heart. We pay attention to it when it is broken or in pain, or impelled by some strong longing, be it for God or someone we love, or even something we desire. The whole goal of the spiritual life can be described as a struggle to purify the heart with God's grace and by honest attempts at self-knowledge and discipline, which cleanse our hearts from unworthy or disordered attachments and desires.

Gradually, very gradually, we come to have a purer heart with less junk and garbage, more and more uncluttered so that we come, a step at a time, to love God and all whom we love in God. A purer heart can delight in and learn from more and more people and more and more things. We begin to love (a little bit) in God and to enjoy so many things that He has given us to use. Mirrors of God become more and more common in the inner landscape of our experience.

As our minds are fed on the teaching of Scripture and the pronouncements of the Church, the whole world of experience slowly takes on the aspect of a great library filled with innumerable books of sacred teachings. All this happens very slowly and painfully, but it happens if we are willing to let it happen and not to let our pet ideas stand in the way. One actually begins to listen to God.

It is very important to realize that only a saint does this listening perfectly, and that many poor suffering sinners do it a little bit, now and then. What is really tragic is that it never happens at all to some people, even some religious people. They don't grow. I've met people who said their prayers, even in cloisters, but they never kept quiet and listened to God. They are afraid to suffer so that they are afraid to rejoice. They never die to themselves so that they never live to themselves. They may pursue a great cause, a great work, or a spiritual goal, but they are never poor enough in their own heart to surrender to God, but only to their narrow images of Him.

This article is supposed to be on how I pray now.

As I read over the lines I have just written, I think, "Good heavens, I don't want to create the illusion that I pray like this. It would be very hypocritical." But to tell the truth, sometimes I do pray like this, but just a little bit. And even on rare days (usually dark days) a little bit more. And if I have any prayer for myself, it is that I may purify my heart so that it has less junk and that I may see clearly around me the mirrors of God, especially in the suffering and the needy. I hope that I may read more deeply in the books of holy teaching that are found lying helter-skelter in the huge library that we call daily life.

We are told in the Bible, "Be still, and know that I am God" (Psalm 46:10). This is absolutely the best method of prayer. I regret that it took me half a century to realize the profound truth in this summons of God Himself. I am filled with gratitude that at last I have learned this truth, at least a little bit.

Father Benedict J. Groeschel, C.F.R., a psychologist and spiritual director, directs the office for spiritual development of the Archdiocese of New York.

Our Sunday Visitor...
Your Source for Discovering the Riches of the Catholic Faith

Our Sunday Visitor has an extensive line of materials for young children, teens, and adults. Our books, Bibles, booklets, CD-ROMs, audios, and videos are available in bookstores worldwide.

To receive a FREE full-line catalog or for more information, call **Our Sunday Visitor** at **1-800-348-2440**. Or write, **Our Sunday Visitor** / 200 Noll Plaza / Huntington, IN 46750.

Please send me: __ A catalog
Please send me materials on:
   __ Apologetics and catechetics   __ Reference works
   __ Prayer books   __ Heritage and the saints
   __ The family   __ The parish

Name_____
Address_____Apt._____
City_____State___Zip_____
Telephone (   )_____

                                                      A73BBABP

Please send a friend: __ A catalog
Please send a friend materials on:
   __ Apologetics and catechetics   __ Reference works
   __ Prayer books   __ Heritage and the saints
   __ The family   __ The parish

Name_____
Address_____Apt._____
City_____State___Zip_____
Telephone (   )_____

                                                      A73BBABP

Our Sunday Visitor
200 Noll Plaza
Huntington, IN 46750
1-800-348-2440
OSVSALES@AOL.COM

Your Source for Discovering the Riches of the Catholic Faith